VISUAL BASIC

Introduction to Programming
2nd Edition

FRANS VAN WYK

Visual Basic.
Introduction to Programming (2nd Edition)
Copyright © **2019** by Frans Van Wyk
All Rights Reserved
Good Luck!
Frans Van Wyk

LEGAL NOTICE

Table of Contents

Foreword...*1*

    Interesting...4

CHAPTER 1...*5*

  Introduction..5

    Interesting...7

    The Z3 Computer built by Konrad Zuse..7

    The Atanasoff-Berry Computer (ABC)...8

CHAPTER 2...*9*

  Programming Languages...9

  Compilers and Interpreters..12

    Note...12

CHAPTER 3...*15*

  Programming Principles...15

    Flowchart...17

CHAPTER 4...*19*

  Data Types...19

    Primitive data types are divided as:...19

    Non-primitive data types are divided as:..19

    VB primitive types, with the range of values it can contain:.............20

  Variables and constants..22

    Variables: (Can change during runtime) 23

    Constants: (Cannot change during runtime)....................................24

    Return values and parameters:..24

  Types of variables..24

    Numeric Variables...25

    Program: Numeric Variables Example..25

    Output: Numeric Variables Example..26

    Alphanumeric Variables..26

    Program: Alphanumeric Variables Example.....................................27

Output: Alphanumeric Variables Example 27

Other Types of Variables 28

Program: Other Variables Example 28

Output: Other Variables Example 29

Discussion: Other Variables 29

Namespaces **30**

Classes **31**

Program: Class Example 32

Output: Class Example 34

Explanation of Child Class 34

Explanation of StringTest Class 35

Objects **37**

Procedures **38**

Program: Procedure Example 40

Discussion: Procedures Example 41

Discussion: Module ConsoleSetup 43

Output: Procedure Example Without Call 43

Scope 44

Program: Scope Example 44

Discussion: Scope Example 46

Output: Produced After Changes: 48

CHAPTER 5 .... **49**

Control Structures **49**

Sequence **50**

Diagram of Sequential Statements 50

Program: Sequence Example 51

Selection **52**

Diagram of Selection Statements 52

Generic Syntax of the If Statement 53

Multiline syntax: 53

Single-line syntax: 53

Discussion of the parts of each statement. 53

Program: Selection Example 54

Output: Selection Example 55

Iteration **57**

Diagram of Iteration 57

Program: Example of a DO WHILE Loop 58

Discussion: Do Loop Example 60

Different Do Loops: a Quick Peek 60

While/Until 60

The parts of a Do Loop 61

The For Loop 62

Program: The For Loop Example 63

Discussion: For Loop Example 64

Interesting 65

Interesting – Grace Murray Hopper 66

CHAPTER 6.. **67**

Storing and Retrieving Data **67**

Database Example 67

File Example 68

File Handling **68**

Program: File Handling Example 69

Output: File Handling Example 70

Discussion: File Handling Example 71

CHAPTER 7.. **73**

Operators **73**

Arithmetic Operators 73

Comparison Operators 77

Logical Operators 77

Operator Precedence 78

Assignment Operators 79

Programming Quotes 80

CHAPTER 8.. **81**

Arrays **81**

Program: Arrays Example 83

Output: Arrays Example 85

Discussion: Arrays Example 86

Some more examples. 87

Program: Arrays 1 Example 87

Output: Arrays 1 Example 89

Discussion: Arrays 1 Example 89

Program: Arrays Example 91

Output: Arrays Example 92

Discussion: Arrays Example 93

Program: Arrays 2 Example 93

Output: Arrays 2 Example 95

Discussion: Arrays 2 Example 96

Program: Sort Example 98

Output: Sort Example 100

Discussion: Sort Example 100

Fun Facts 102

CHAPTER 9 .... *103*

Programming 103

Getting Started With Visual Studio Community 2019 104

Program: Read Write Example 111

Output: Read Write Example 112

Discussion: Read Write Example 113

Program: Read Multiply and Display Example 114

Output: Read Multiply and Display Example 115

Discussion: Read Multiply and Display Example 116

Program: File Handling Example 118

Output: File Handling Example 120

Discussion: File Handling Example 120

Program: Read and Write Sequential File Example 123

Output 1: Read and Write Sequential File Example 125

Output 2: Read and Write Sequential File Example 126

Discussion: Read and Write Sequential File Example 126

Discussion: Code Segment: 128

CHAPTER 10 .... **133**

Calling External Programs **133**

Using the Windows Shell 133

Output 1: Windows Shell – Printing to Printer 137

Printing Contents Shown in Notepad 137

Discussion: Windows Shell – Printing to Printer 137

Program Segment: Class WindowsShell 139

Output: Sub OpenCmd() (Shown in Notepad) 140

Discussion: Program Segment Class WindowsShell 141

Output: Sub OpenEdge() 142

Discussion: Open Edge Example 143

Using external objects **144**

Output: The Interface 149

Discussion: The Interface 149

Syntax for the select case statement 151

Discussion: Word Example 153

Output: Word - When File Exists 155

Output: Word - When File Does Not Exist 156

Discussion: Excel Example 156

Output: Excel Example 158

Discussion: Powerpoint Example 158

Output: Example.pptx before slides are added 159

Output: Example.pptx after slides are added 160

Output: Blank Powerpoint Example 161

Visual Studio IDE 162

CHAPTER 11 .... **163**

Forms Applications **163**

Introduction 163

List of Common Controls 164

Example of a Form With Most Common Controls 166

Now let us see this in action. 167

Insert code in buttons. 174

The unmarked code.. 179

Text To Speech Forms Example **180**

Program: Text to Speech Example... 181

Discussion: Text to Speech Example... 184

List of Values for Message Dialogue 188

Conclusion.. **190**

Appendix A...*191*

Install Visual Studio 2019 191

Step 1 - Make sure your computer is ready for Visual Studio............................ 191

Before you begin installing Visual Studio: 191

Step 2 - Download Visual Studio... 192

Step 3 - Install the Visual Studio installer 192

Step 4 - Choose workloads 193

Step 5 - Select individual components (Optional).. 194

Step 6 - Install language packs (Optional) 195

Change the installer language from the command line 195

Step 7 - Change the installation location (Optional) 196

Important... 196

Step 8 - Start developing.. 197

Glossary *199*

Index *225*

ACKNOWLEDGMENTS

Firstly, I must acknowledge my wife Rina for her support through the years, even if she calls the computer my first wife.

Secondly, a big salute to Ed Dale, Dan Raine and the Thirty Day Challenge team for showing me the way.

FOREWORD

A little bit of background about me would be in order here, I think.

I've been a lecturer in Information Technology at the Central University of Technology, Free State, in South Africa for 27 years. Before that, I spent years in the industry in various capacities.

During all these years, I programmed and taught in quite a lot of computer languages for both mainframe systems and desktop computers. Well, calling the Sinclair  ZX81, with its 1 Kilobyte (yes, you've read that correctly) internal memory, a desktop computer is stretching it a bit. Progressed through the ranks with a  Commodore 64 (38911 bytes free after loading its mother tongue Basic) Apple's IIe and MacBook, Pc's (XT, AT, and the rest) up to today's PC desktop, which is actually more powerful than a 1970's mainframe. Yes, I have worked on, but not owned, mini as well as mainframe computers.

Programming for that lot included Minimal Basic, Commodore Basic, and the rest of the Basic versions up to Visual Basic .Net, COBOL (COmmon Business Oriented Language), Algol, FORTRAN, Pascal, Delphi and even an obscure language called MOBOL. The latter was a language used on Mohawk Computers (It later became Bull Computers). The acronym stands for Mohawk Business Oriented Language. I ended up with C# and Microsoft Visual Basic for the .Net framework.

I taught Development Software II, III and IV, Advanced Development Software IV, Information Systems, Software Engineering III and IV, Systems Software, and Research Methodology, to name but a few.

Phew! I'm even getting tired from naming them all.

From the above, you should by now have figured out I love computers as well as teaching. During my time as a lecturer, I found that many times, people are apprehensive about C#, because of the C and C++ legacy. Especially C++, because of its notoriety as being very difficult to master.

Well, I think this Introduction to Programming in Visual Basic will show that Visual Basic is not difficult to master at all.

I hope you enjoy reading the book just as much as I've enjoyed writing it.

Frans Van Wyk

PS: Get your Free Code here: https://mailchi.mp/8bbe355fe540/vb-book-code

WELCOME TO THE WORLD OF

Interesting

(Adapted from Wikipedia).

Most first-generation BASIC versions supported simple data types, loop cycles, and arrays. The following example is written for GW-BASIC, but will work in most versions of BASIC with minimal changes:

```
10 INPUT "What is your name: "; U$
20 PRINT "Hello "; U$

30 INPUT "How many stars do you want: "; N
40 S$ = ""
50 FOR I = 1 TO N
60 S$ = S$ + "*"
70 NEXT I
80 PRINT S$
90 INPUT "Do you want more stars? "; A$
100 IF LEN(A$) = 0 THEN GOTO 90
110 A$ = LEFT$(A$, 1)
120 IF A$ = "Y" OR A$ = "y" THEN GOTO 30
130 PRINT "Goodbye "; U$
140 END
```

The resulting dialog might resemble:

```
What is your name: Mike
Hello Mike
How many stars do you want: 7
*******

Do you want more stars? yes
How many stars do you want: 3
***

Do you want more stars? no
Goodbye Mike
```

CHAPTER 1

INTRODUCTION

Visual Basic is one of the newer programming languages, called an **object oriented language**. This means that we see everything that's going to be in our system, and that we want to use and carry data for, as an object. It may

not even be a physical object, like a person or a horse. It can be something that can only exist in a digital world, like a sound, or a picture, or a combination of things like a booking on a plane. The important thing here is that we must carry data for it. An object has characteristics, like eye color, name, etc. We call those characteristics, attributes.

Doing something with the object, like read, write etc. is accomplished by procedures or functions which VB refers to as Methods.

A **procedure** can be thought of as a task to be done. You can switch on your electric light without knowing anything about the electrons moving around, or whatever makes electricity flow. You just have to know that if you flip the switch the light must come on, or if the light is on when you flip it, it should go off. If it doesn't there's an error somewhere. In just the same way you only have to know what the procedure is going to do, to use it. We call that principle "information hiding" or "encapsulation".

If we want to pass data over to the procedure, we use parameters which contain the data needed by the procedure to do its job. The inner workings of the procedure is hidden from us. Just like, for instance, we send a manuscript to the printers without caring how they do the job. We only want our printed book back.

The objects can later communicate in a certain way to accomplish a variety of actions.

The object is an instance of a class. The class contains the structure of the object, as a blueprint contains the map for building a house, for example. You can use that blueprint to build many houses and sell them to different people. The blueprint tells you what the house should look like (the class) and each house represents an instance of that class, in other words the object.

Each instance of an object has its own data associated with it. One house's owner may be Charles, and another house's owner Anne. The amount each must still pay will be incorporated in that specific owner's account (object instance). These objects can then be stored in an appropriate file or database for later use.

Microsoft Visual Studio is an Integrated Development Environment (IDE) that we can use to create all these objects with their data structures and procedures. There are also free environments to download. We will look at a few of these later.

There are ways to store and retrieve the data and present it to the user.

Data can be entered in many ways, for example, with the keyboard. It can also be presented in different ways like on the screen or printed in a report.

As far as Information Technology is concerned there is a difference between data and information. **Data** can be anything we use that will not necessarily have any meaning when not put into context. **Information** have meaning and can be understood by us humans.

Obviously, there's much more to programming than stated above, and we'll look at these in the rest of the book.

Interesting
The Z3 Computer built by Konrad Zuse

The Z3, an early computer built by German engineer Konrad Zuse working in complete isolation from developments elsewhere, uses 2,300 relays, performs floating point binary arithmetic, and has a 22-bit word length. The Z3 was used for aerodynamic calculations but was destroyed in a bombing raid on Berlin in late 1943. Zuse later supervised a reconstruction of the Z3 in the 1960s, which is currently on display at the Deutsches Museum in Munich.

The Atanasoff-Berry Computer (ABC)

After successfully demonstrating a proof-of-concept prototype in 1939, Professor John Vincent Atanasoff receives funds to build a full-scale machine at Iowa State College (now University). The machine was designed and built by Atanasoff and graduate student Clifford Berry between 1939 and 1942. The ABC was at the center of a patent dispute related to the invention of the computer, which was resolved in 1973 when it was shown that ENIAC co-designer John Mauchly had seen the ABC shortly after it became functional.

The legal result was a landmark: Atanasoff was declared the originator of several basic computer ideas, but the computer as a concept was declared un-patentable and thus freely open to all. A full-scale working replica of the ABC was completed in 1997, proving that the ABC machine functioned as Atanasoff had claimed. The replica is currently on display at the Computer History Museum. https://www.computerhistory.org/timeline/computers/

CHAPTER 2

PROGRAMMING LANGUAGES

A **programming language** is a set of commands, instructions, and other syntax used to create a software program. This is done through the use of syntactic and semantic rules, to determine structure and meaning respectively. The computer is a dumb machine and will do very little without being instructed to. The set of instructions we give to the computer to enable it to do a certain task, is called **a program**.

A very small example that displays "Goodbye Cruel World" on the screen (console) could look like this:

```
Namespace World
    Class World
        Shared Sub Main()
            'A small console program in VB
            Console.WriteLine("Goodbye Cruel World")
            Console.ReadKey()
        End Sub
    End Class
End Namespace
```

Programs that are more elaborate use Forms (like the following example) to create a more sophisticated user interface:

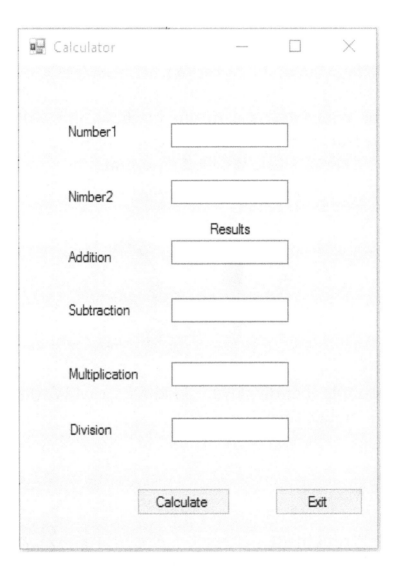

The code to create this very simple calculator looks as follows:

```vb
Public Class frmCalculator
    Dim Num1, Num2, Result As Integer
    Dim Result1 As Double

        Private Sub Button1_Click(sender As
                        System.Object, e As
                        System.EventArgs) Handles Button1.Click
            Num1 = TextBox1.Text
            Num2 = TextBox2.Text
            Result = Num1 + Num2
            TextBox3.Text = Result
            Result = Num1 - Num2
            TextBox4.Text = Result
            Result = Num1 * Num2
            TextBox5.Text = Result
            Result1 = Num1 / Num2
            TextBox6.Text = Result1.ToString("N3")
        End Sub

        Private Sub Button2_Click(sender As Object, e As EventArgs)  Handles
                            Button2.Click
            Me.Close()
        End Sub
End Class
```

COMPILERS AND INTERPRETERS

Before we can jump in and start programming, it would be advisable to say something about compilers and interpreters.

A computer, as you know by now, is only a machine that follows instructions. We saw that the instructions are in the form of code written in a programming language. That's all good and well, but there's one snag. The computer can only work with electronic circuits that's either on or off. That means it has only two states. In computer jargon, we call such a small on/off component a bit.

Because of having two states only, we say that if the component is on it represents a 1, and if it's off it represents a 0. A numbering system like that, which has only two digits, is called a binary system. To have only zeros and ones to work with creates difficulties, because with such a system there are only two possibilities, 0 or 1. Obviously, it is really difficult, almost impossible, to write and debug a program while using only two characters. To overcome this problem the computer uses a combination of zeros and ones to represent a character.

Note

The binary system refers to the way numbers are represented for use in computers. Only two symbols (**0 & 1**) are employed to write these numbers, with their positional notation determining their meaning. The binary system is a *base two* system.

The expression of the system is generally formulated in relation to the progression of powers of 2.

The progression of powers for the number two produces the progression of a constant number series:

$2^0 = 1$, $2^1 = 2$, $2^2 = 4$, $2^3 = 8$, $2^4 = 16$, $2^5 = 32$, $2^6 = 64$, $2^7 = 128$, $2^8 = 256$, etc.

Using the binary system of notation, then **1011** $= 1(2^3) + 0(2^2) + 1(2) + 1$.

In other words, the decimal equivalent of the aforementioned is 8+0+2+1 = 11 in decimal.

If we have 2 bits, we can have 4 possibilities:

Both bits on=11, both off=00, and then two others namely 10 and 01.

The option of representing 4 characters is not very useful at all, so some codes were created to represent more characters. One of the earliest is called ASCII (pronounce "as-key") and later Unicode that can represent many more characters. We use these codes to represent characters in the computer.

In that way, we can store any number of combinations (actually as many as the internal memory would allow). Obviously, our program statements are also groups of these characters and thus groups of zeros and ones. That is the only way the program can be executed on the computer. So firstly, the statements in VB, that we can understand, must be converted to a number of zeros and ones that the computer can understand. We call this transformation, compiling. In this process, the whole program is compiled into the zeros and ones that is called machine code. The machine code is the only code that can be executed. The program that does this conversion is called a **compiler**.

With the compiler, all the code is compiled before we can see if everything is correct. We can actually compile statement by statement and report back after each statement to see if that is correct. This we call an **interpreter**. It is not necessary for the scope of this book to go further into these processes, but it should be obvious that we need either a compiler, or an interpreter, or a combination to convert our high-level computer language (VB) into executable machine code.

As far as VB is concerned, we have a few options for a compiler. The most obvious is Microsoft Visual Studio, because Microsoft created the language VB to be used on its .Net platform. Unfortunately, this package is very expensive. Visual Studio is, however, not necessary for just getting to know the basics of VB.

Fortunately, there is a free option namely Visual Studio Community. It is free and can be downloaded from the link below:

https://www.visualstudio.com/vs/community/

NB. See the instructions to get Visual Studio Community installed on your computer in Appendage A.

CHAPTER 3

PROGRAMMING PRINCIPLES

First of all, we must distinguish between two very important principles, namely semantics and syntax. **Semantics** refers to the meaning of what we say, while **syntax** refers to how we say it. For instance; if I say "the chair walks", it is syntactically correct, because the rule in English says that if the object is referred to in the third person, and singular, the verb must take an "s" at the end. Therefore, we're syntactically correct. Semantically that would be

totally wrong and meaningless, because a chair can't walk. Well except if you have been smoking something really weird.

When writing **a program**, you must first figure out what you want to do, and then you can write the statements to accomplish that. In other words, you must have a plan to work from. That plan is called an **algorithm** and consists of the detailed steps to accomplish something.

Let's say we want to find the highest number in a list of numbers. One would say, "Well that's easy, go through the list and pick the highest number". That's perfectly understandable for us humans, but remember, the computer is a machine. It doesn't have an instinctive insight of the problem based on previous experience. We must tell it precisely, step-by-step what to do. Let's assume there will be at least one number.

Therefore, we would have to say something like this:

❖ Create a space in memory to store the highest number. Call it HighestNumber
❖ Get the first number
❖ Keep it in memory in HighestNumber
❖ Are there more numbers? [3]
  ➢ *Yes*
    ▪ Get the next number
    ▪ Compare it to HighestNumber
      • Is it greater than the number in HighestNumber?
      • *Yes*
        ♦ ***Store the new number in HighestNumber***
        ♦ Go back to the third step [3]
      • *No*
      • Go back to the third step [3]
  ➢ *No*
  ➢ Stop
❖ The highest number is in HighestNumber

This is just an example of how a human will get the highest number. It is, however, inadequate for a computer. We will need a few extra steps if we want to write the code for a program to find the highest number. As you will see later, in programming there are only three structures we may use, and the algorithm above does not adhere to that structures.

We can also use a flowchart like in the next example to show the steps.

Flowchart.

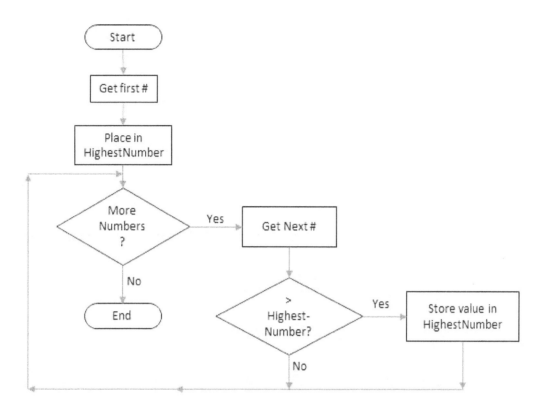

When we start writing code there are some things to keep in mind. Let's look at the bit of code below:

```vb
Namespace World
  Class World
    Shared Sub Main()
      'A small console program in VB 1
      Console.WriteLine("Goodbye Cruel World")
      Console.ReadKey()
    End Sub
  End Class
End Namespace
```

As you can see, the different statement groups are indented. This makes the code much easier to read and helps when someone must maintain the code. Learn how to use white space in your code to help with readability. Luckily, the IDE in Visual Studio makes it easier by doing most of the indenting automatically. White space is your own responsibility. Continue code on a new line where it makes sense and the code easier to read.

A very important principle is to use comments in your code to explain what you're doing. Remember, it's not always you that have to maintain the code. Even if it is you, the probability that you will remember what you were doing a few months down the line is very slim.

A comment is preceded by a single quotation mark '. The line in green in the code on the previous page is a comment[1]. In visual Basic all the characters on the same line after the apostrophe sign (') is ignored by the compiler.

CHAPTER 4

DATA TYPES

As you will remember, data is the characters that we want to use in our system. In other words, the quantities, characters, or symbols on which operations are performed by a computer. Obviously, there are different data types we can use, like characters, numbers etc.

There are some types that have been predefined by the programming language/computer, and usually cannot be broken down further into components. These are called primitive types.

Primitive data types are divided as:

Byte, Sbyte, Short, Ushort, Integer, Uinteger, Long, Ulong, Single, Double, Decimal, Char, Boolean, Date, String, Object.

We can define other types by combining different primitive types to store complex data structures. For example, an address that consist of the street name, street number, city, postal code etc. Although it consists of different primitive types, it belongs together and can be referred to with a single name.

Non-primitive data types are divided as:

Class, Structure, Enum, Interface, Delegate, Array

VB primitive types, with the range of values it can contain:

Visual Basic type	Common language runtime type structure	Nominal storage allocation	Value range
Boolean	Boolean	Depends on implementing platform	True or False
Byte	Byte	1 byte	0 through 255 (unsigned)
Char (single character)	Char	2 bytes	0 through 65535 (unsigned)
Date	DateTime	8 bytes	0:00:00 (midnight) on January 1, 0001 through 11:59:59 PM on December 31, 9999
Decimal	Decimal	16 bytes	0 through +/-79,228,162,514,264,337,593,543,950,335 (+/-7.9...E+28) [†] with no decimal point; 0 through +/-7.9228162514264337593543950335 with 28 places to the right of the decimal; smallest nonzero number is +/-0.0000000000000000000000000001 (+/-1E-28) [†]
Double (double-precision floating-point)	Double	8 bytes	-1.79769313486231570E+308 through -4.94065645841246544E-324 [†] for negative values; 4.94065645841246544E-324 through 1.79769313486231570E+308 [†] for positive values
Integer	Int32	4 bytes	-2,147,483,648 through 2,147,483,647 (signed)
Long (long integer)	Int64	8 bytes	-9,223,372,036,854,775,808 through 9,223,372,036,854,775,807 (9.2...E+18 [†]) (signed)

Object	Object (class)	4 bytes on 32-bit platform 8 bytes on 64-bit platform	Any type can be stored in a variable of type Object
SByte	SByte	1 byte	-128 through 127 (signed)
Short (short integer)	Int16	2 bytes	-32,768 through 32,767 (signed)
Single (single-precision floating-point)	Single	4 bytes	-3.4028235E+38 through -1.401298E-45 * for negative values; 1.401298E-45 through 3.4028235E+38 * for positive values
String (variable-length)	String (class)	Depends on implementing platform	0 to approximately 2 billion Unicode characters
UInteger	UInt32	4 bytes	0 through 4,294,967,295 (unsigned)
ULong	UInt64	8 bytes	0 through 18,446,744,073,709,551,615 (1.8...E+19 *) (unsigned)
User-Defined (structure)	(inherits from ValueType)	Depends on implementing platform	Each member of the structure has a range determined by its data type and independent of the ranges of the other members
UShort	UInt16	2 bytes	0 through 65,535 (unsigned)

In *scientific notation*, "E" refers to a power of 10. So 3.56E+2 signifies 3.56×10^2 or 356, and 3.56E-2 signifies $3.56 / 10^2$ or 0.0356.

VARIABLES AND CONSTANTS

The computer architecture usually consists of the Central Processing Unit (CPU), internal and external memory, as well as Peripherals that refer to external devices like a printer, scanner, etc.

The CPU is the boss and manages the work (at least as far as programming goes) by making use of a special type of program called the Operating System.

Internal memory resides in the memory area of the computer and data are kept there only temporarily.

The external memory stores data outside of the CPU and internal memory. It can be in the form of some sort of storing device like a hard disk, or a USB memory stick etc.

Before **a program** can be executed, the statements must first be loaded into a part of internal memory. Any data that we want to use for calculations, presentations etc. must also first be entered into memory. Maybe through a keyboard, from a storage device, or from some other capturing device.

To access any data in memory there must be a name associated with the memory location where the data are stored. We call these memory locations, cells. Obviously, it would be very difficult to keep track of where the data are placed after it was entered. We poor humans find it very difficult to remember the numbers, which are called addresses, and refers to the

memory cell where the data is stored. Luckily for us, the Operating System keeps track of the physical locations and the moving of the data in and out of memory and the CPU.

We will not be going into all the intricacies of storage and memory but, suffice it to say, it would be easier for us to give a certain piece of memory a meaningful name, like First Name, Last Name etc. Then we can tell the program, via instructions, to use the data in the cell associated with that name. The contents of that cell or number of cells are then available for whatever we want to do with it. The analogy usually used is that of a postbox. There is, however, an important difference. You can put more than one letter in a postbox, but anything you put in a memory cell overwrites the item currently there.

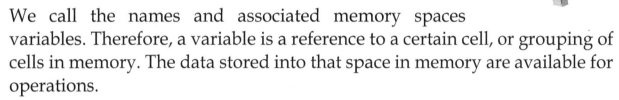

We call the names and associated memory spaces variables. Therefore, a variable is a reference to a certain cell, or grouping of cells in memory. The data stored into that space in memory are available for operations.

Any of the types shown under Data Types can be used to specify what values a variable can contain. In a language like VB, all variables must be declared before it can be used and can consist of any of the data types we have seen in the previous section.

We accomplish the creation of variables with declaration statements, which name the variable, and specifies what type it is.

Variables: (Can change during runtime)

```
Dim answer As Integer = 42
Dim greeting AS string = "Hi World!"
```

We use the Dim statement to declare a variable, and the As statement to specify the type. The type can be any of the data types we stated in the previous section.

The declaration Dim answer As Integer = 42, declares a variable with the name *answer* as type Integer, and assigns a value of 42 to it. Because the variable is declared as Integer, we can only assign numeric values to it. The = sign is used to assign a value to a variable, or for comparison. More about comparison later.

The declaration Dim greeting AS string = "Hi World!", declares the variable *greeting* as String and assigns the value "Hi World" to it. Because the variable is declared as String, we can only assign an alphanumeric value to it. OK, we can assign numeric characters to a string type, but then it takes on an alphanumeric type and cannot be used for calculations etc. The value of a string type must be between quotes as shown above.

Constants: (Cannot change during runtime)

```
Const speedLimit As Integer = 120
Const pi As Double = 3.1415926535897931
```

The statement to declare a constant is Const. The rest of the statement works the same as with the Dim statement.

The major difference between the Dim and Const statements is the fact that with a variable declared with Dim we can change the value at any time by assigning a new value to it. With a Const statement a value can only be assigned to it in the declaration statement, and not later in the code.

Return values and parameters:

```
Function AddValues(a As Integer, b As Integer) As Long
    Dim result As Long = a + b
    Return result
End Function
```

Return values and parameters will be discussed later, but was included at this stage for the sake of completeness.

TYPES OF VARIABLES

There are mainly three types of variables, namely Numeric, Alphanumeric and, let us say, Other.

Numeric Variables

Numeric variables can store different types of numeric data, like Integers, which are numbers without a decimal point, or Real numbers, which have decimals.

Program: Numeric Variables Example

```
Namespace NumericVariablesExample
  Class Program
    Shared Sub Main()                          Declaration
      Dim myInt As Integer = 39
      Dim myDbl As Double = 33.999

      SetUpConsole¹("Numeric Variables Example")

      Console.WriteLine(myInt)
      Console.WriteLine(myDbl)
      Console.WriteLine()
      Console.ReadKey()
      myInt = 42                    Use
      myDbl = 1344.14
      Console.WriteLine(myInt)
      Console.WriteLine(myDbl)
      Console.ReadKey()
    End Sub

    Shared Sub SetUpConsole²(Name)
      Console.Title = Name
      Console.BackgroundColor = ConsoleColor.White
```

----

[1] Will be described later
[2] Will be described later

```
      Console.ForegroundColor = ConsoleColor.Black
      Console.Clear()
  End Sub
 End Class
End Namespace
```

Output: Numeric Variables Example

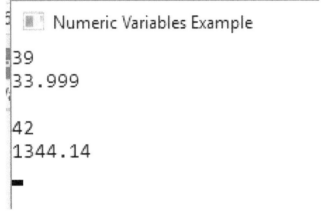

Numeric Variables Example

```
39
33.999

42
1344.14
```

Alphanumeric Variables

Alphanumeric variables store data that are seen as non-numeric. In other words, we can't do any numeric calculations with it. It wouldn't make sense to try to multiply a name by an address. So even if we store the character 1 or 0 in an alphanumeric variable it will still be seen as text, and thus we cannot do mathematical computations on it. For programming purposes, alphanumeric data are shown in quotes. For example, "Hello World".

Program: Alphanumeric Variables Example

```vbnet
Namespace Alpha_Variable_Example
  Class AlphaVariableExample
    Shared Sub Main()
      Dim myString As String = "Hello World"
      SetUpConsole("Alphanumeric Variable Example")
      Console.WriteLine(myString)
      Console.WriteLine()
      Console.ReadKey()
      myString = "Goodbye Cruel World!"
      Console.WriteLine(myString)
      Console.ReadKey()
    End Sub
    Shared Sub SetUpConsole(Name)
      Console.Title = Name
      Console.BackgroundColor = ConsoleColor.White
      Console.ForegroundColor = ConsoleColor.Black
      Console.Clear()
    End Sub
  End Class
End Namespace
```

Output: Alphanumeric Variables Example

```
  ▪  Alpahnumeric Variable Example

Hello World

Goodbye Cruel World!
```

Other Types of Variables

The third category consists of things like objects, which can group a number of different data types.

The Structure Simple statement below creates a structure that includes a combination of three different types of variables.

The application of the statement is shown below.

Program: Other Variables Example

```
01  Namespace Other_Variables_Example
02    Class OtherVariablesExample
03      Structure Simple
04          Public position As Integer
05          Public exists As Boolean
06          Public lastValue As Double
07      End Structure
08
09      Shared Sub Main()
10
11          SetUpConsole("Other Variables Example")
12          Dim s As Simple
13          s.position = 1
14          s.exists = False
15          s.lastValue = 5.5
16          Dim x As Simple
17
18          x = s
19
20          Console.WriteLine("This is X")
```

```
21          Console.WriteLine(x.position)
22          Console.WriteLine(x.exists)
23          Console.WriteLine(x.lastValue)
24          Console.ReadKey()
25      End Sub
26      Shared Sub SetUpConsole(Name)
27          Console.Title = Name
28          Console.BackgroundColor = ConsoleColor.White
29          Console.ForegroundColor = ConsoleColor.Black
30          Console.Clear()
31      End Sub
32    End Class
33  End Namespace
```

Output: Other Variables Example

```
    Other Variables Example

This is X
1
False
5.5
```

Discussion: Other Variables

For this example we'll have to look at some code to explain. **NB.** Remember, the code has been numbered to make the discussion easier.

Let's look at lines 3 to 7 where we use a **structure**. When you declare a **structure**, it becomes a *composite data type*, and you can declare variables of that type. Structures are useful when you want a single variable to hold several related pieces of information.

In line 3 a structure called *Simple* has been declared. Anything between the declaration and the End Structure statement forms part of the structure.

In lines 4, 5 and 6 three variables are declared. The variable in line 5 is declared as type Boolean. In other words, it can receive either true or false as a value.

Ignore line 11, (SetUpConsole("Other Variables Example")), for now. It just changes the Console to display black text on a white background, instead of the other way round.

In line 12 we declare a variable called *s* of the type Simple. That variable can now contain values for the included variables.

In lines 13, 14 and 15 we assign values to the three variables of structure **s**. Notice that we use a period to specify which variable we assign the value to. The statement **s.Position = 1,** assigns a value to the *Position* variable that forms part of the structure **s**.

In line 16 we declare a variable x of the same type as s.

In line 18 we assign the variable **s** to the variable **x**. X now contains the same values as the Structure **s**.

In lines 20 to 23 we write the values of the new structure (x) to the Console.

In line 24 we tell the console to wait for any key to be pressed.

As you can see from the output, x now contains the values we assigned to the variable s.

NAMESPACES

Namespaces are used as an organizational system. They provide a way to classify and present programming elements that are exposed to other programs and applications.

A namespace can be accessed from code anywhere in the same project, from other projects that reference the project, and from libraries containing objects for re-use.

If you do not specify a Namespace for your project, Visual Studio will automatically assign a root Namespace consisting of the name of your project.

We can think of a Namespace in the same way as we think of a folder on the computer. It is essentially used to group related code in a logical way to make it easier to find and use when necessary.

For the scope of this book it isn't necessary to go into namespaces in depth.

Classes

As I have explained already, the main structure for coding is the class. You will remember that a class is the blueprint from which we can create the objects that are instances of that class.

A class also gives us the power to use inheritance and polymorphism. These are very important principles, but beyond the scope of this introductory book. A brief explanation will, however, be in order.

A base class can be created, for instance, Person. We can then specify the main characteristics for a person. Something like Name, Surname, ID Number, Date of birth etc. These are all attributes that a Person can have. Now we can use this base class and create a class Student. A student will inherit all the attributes from the class person, but can also have new attributes like Course, Subjects passed, Moneys owed etc. If we use the class person, we can also create a class lecturer. Lecturer will inherit all the properties from Person again, but we can now specify new properties that are unique to Lecturer. Something like Class schedule, Salary, Personnel number etc. This

helps to create code that we can use again, without specifying the shared properties.

The other principle we spoke about is polymorphism, which literally means, many shapes. Here we can have a class that, for instance, calculates the circumference of a shape. Say we pass one value to the class, that value will be multiplied by 4 to give the circumference of a square. If we pass two parameters, it will multiply the one number by 2, do the same for the other number, and add them together to give the circumference of a rectangle. In that way, we can have one class that does the calculation but uses different methods inside the class. This also helps with the reuse of code.

There are certain classes in VB that have been predefined and stored in libraries. These we can just use without coding it again. We can, however, create our own classes to do whatever we want it to do.

Program: Class Example

```
Namespace ClassExample
    Class Child
        Private age As Integer
        Private name As String
        'Default constructor
        Public Sub New()
            name = "N/A"
        End Sub
        'Constructor
        Public Sub New(name As String, age As Integer)
            Me.name = name
            Me.age = age
        End Sub
        'Printing method
        Public Sub PrintChild()
            Console.WriteLine("{0}, {1} years old.", name, age)
        End Sub
    End Class 'Child
```

```vbnet
Class StringTest
    Shared Sub Main()
        'Create objects by using the new operator
        Dim child1 As Child = New Child("Craig", 11)
        Dim child2 As Child = New Child("Sally", 10)
        'Create object using the default constructor
        Dim child3 As Child = New Child()

        SetUpConsole("ClassExample Example")

        'Display results
        Console.Write("Child #1: ")
        child1.PrintChild()
        Console.Write("Child #2: ")
        child2.PrintChild()
        Console.Write("Child #3: ")
        child3.PrintChild()
        Console.ReadKey()
    End Sub

    Shared Sub SetUpConsole(Name)
        Console.Title = Name
        Console.BackgroundColor = ConsoleColor.White
        Console.ForegroundColor = ConsoleColor.Black
        Console.Clear()
    End Sub
End Class
End Namespace
```

Output: Class Example

```
   ClassExample Example
Child #1: Craig, 11 years old.
Child #2: Sally, 10 years old.
Child #3: N/A, 0 years old.
```

Explanation of Child Class

Class Child Creates a class called Child.

Private age As Integer Declares an integer variable, which is only available in the class. You will see we used Private instead of Dim.

Private name As String Declares a string variable which is also private.

The next three lines declares the default constructor.

```
Public Sub New()
    name = "N/A"
End Sub
```

A constructor is always called New(). This constructor will be used when we call the class without parameters, as in the third Dim statement in the class *StringTest* on page 33. Because we don't supply a parameter for the name, it will automatically use "N/A".

The next four lines declares a constructor with two parameters.

```
Public Sub New(name As String, age As Integer)
    Me.name = name
    Me.age = age
End Sub
```

When a constructor will be called with one or more parameters, that parameters must be declared with a name and a type.

In the instance as shown, the class is called with the two parameters. The first value will be assigned to the name property, and the second to the age property. Because the variables *name* and *age* (with their types) are included in the parameter list, it is not necessary to declare them in the constructor. These variables will contain the values passed to them through the parameters included in the call statement. As you can see, we assign these parameter variables to the properties (also called attributes) *name* and *age* in the constructor. The keyword Me, refers to the procedure in which it resides.

The next three lines declares a method called PrintChild() to display the values of the properties on the console.

```
Public Sub PrintChild()
    Console.WriteLine("{0},{1} years old.", name, age)
End Sub
```

The statement Console.WriteLine("{0},{1} years old.", name, age) will write the values of the variables name and age to the console. You will see that the quoted string, "{0},{1} years old." looks really funny with the curly brackets included. There is, however, method to our madness. Here we are including place holders in the string separated by a comma. In this case, there are two placeholders. When we use the string, we must include the values we want to use in the placeholders, as we have done with the name and age as parameters after the closing quote in the statement.

Explanation of StringTest Class

The StringTest class is our main class that contains the compulsory Sub Main().

```
Dim child1 As Child = New Child("Craig", 11) and
Dim child2 As Child = New Child("Sally", 10) create two instances of the
```
Child class with properties for Name and Age. The instantiation of the two objects is achieved with the New statement.

Dim child3 As Child = New Child() creates an instance of child, but without properties. Because of this, the default constructer of Child is called and the name "N/A" is supplied.

The next six lines print the detail of each Child object (remember an instance of a class is called an object) to the console.

```
Console.Write("Child #1: ")
child1.PrintChild()
Console.Write("Child #2: ")
child2.PrintChild()
Console.Write("Child #3: ")
child3.PrintChild()

Console.ReadKey()
```

Console.Write writes directly to the console whereas child1.PrintChild() uses the PrintChild method of the Child class to print to the console.

Console.Write prints the value(s) stated in the parameter to the console, but stays on the same line, whereas Console.WriteLine prints the value(s) stated in the parameter but moves to a new line after printing. (WriteLine is used in the PrintChild method.)

Just to refresh your memory; the output looks like this:

```
ClassExample Example

Child #1: Craig, 11 years old.
Child #2: Sally, 10 years old.
Child #3: N/A, 0 years old.
```

OBJECTS

What is an object? As stated in the introduction an object is anything that plays a role in our system and that we want to carry data for.

That definition is not strictly correct, as an object in programming terms, is an instance of a class. The class is the blueprint remember, and the object is an instance of the class. The class is the plan and the object is whatever we created from the plan.

What forms part of an object? First of all, we have to describe the object in terms of how it's going to look, in other words its characteristics. What do we want the object to contain as variables, and what actions must the object be able to take on those contents? The actions will be done by methods.

An object has storage for everything it should act upon, as well as the actions to be carried out. Just as a normal world object has some characteristics like eye color, hair color, gender etc. the programming object has attributes (also called properties) that describe it. Sorage will be in the form of variables declared in the class. By specifying what data an object may accept, we are protecting the object against some unwanted values that it may not be able to work with.

Objects communicate with each other by sending messages. Sounds weird, but the messages are only values that we sent to the object in the form of the contents of variables, or literal values. When the object is defined, we must specify what data it can accept, and in what form. We send the data through parameters. A parameter can contain a variable, for instance, FirstName. It then passes the contents of FirstName, for example "Frank", to the object. A literal value would be something like 123.44, or "Hi there".

In the same fashion we must specify, with the structure of the methods incorporated, what actions the object can execute. For example, we can specify a method to save data in a database, but not a method to delete the data. In that way we can make sure that the object cannot produce unexpected, unwanted results.

Look at the next example. It uses the same object that was explained in the previous example.

We will use the blueprint of the **class "Child"** and create instances of the object for each of the two times we used the "**New**" keyword.

```
Dim child1 As Child = New Child("Craig", 11)
Dim child2 As Child = New Child("Sally", 10)
```

In other words, it creates an instance for each of child1 and child2, and pass the literal values to the constructor we created in:

```
Public Sub New(name As String, age As Integer)
    Me.name = name
    Me.age = age
End Sub
```

When we instantiate an object from the class, the values for each property are passed through the parameters between brackets:

```
New (name As String, age As Integer)
```

As we have seen in the explanation, these values can then be used in the instance of the object. Remember that each time we used the New keyword to create an object, the values are specific to that instance.

PROCEDURES

In programming languages, a procedure can be seen as a collection of code that belongs and works together to accomplish one outcome. Not one thing as in 2+3=5, but one procedure as, for example, in reading data from the console, processing it, and saving the information to a hard drive. Some programming languages have a type of procedure called a function. The only difference between a procedure and a function is the fact that a function can return a value to the caller, and the procedure not.

The caller is the "container" from where the procedure/function is called. (Remember the notorious line SetupConsole with a parameter we said we'll look at later.)

Because a function returns a value it must reside at the right of the "=" sign in a statement.

For example, Salary = CalcSal(hours, overtime)

In VB, there are two types of methods (procedures); sub procedures and functions. The sub procedure cannot return a value. If we want to return a value, it must be declared as a function, and can be declared as being of a certain type. A Function must also have a Return statement in the body.

Both Methods and Functions can have parameters that may receive values from the caller. Parameters are specified when the Method or Function is declared and appear between brackets in the header. When such a procedure is called, values must be supplied for the parameters.

Procedure   **Function**

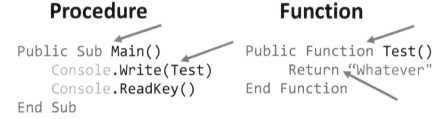

```
Public Sub Main()               Public Function Test()
    Console.Write(Test)             Return "Whatever"
    Console.ReadKey()           End Function
End Sub
```

Methods and Functions are used to enable code to be reused, and to group statements that belong together to stay together. It is also easier to program if you just have to keep a certain subset of ideas in mind. That again adheres to the principle of hiding the complexity. Just as the class groups the attributes and methods together, the method keeps statements that belong together in one block of code.

- Every method must have a name and must be inside a class or a structure.
- If the method is to be available in the rest of the program, it must be declared as public.

- Every VB program has at least one class or module with a method named Main().

Program: Procedure Example

NB. In this example, the lines have been numbered to make explaining the code easier. It does not form part of the code.

```
01  Namespace ProcedureExample
02      Public Class ProgramMethod
03          Public Sub ProcedureExample()
04              Console.WriteLine()
05              Console.WriteLine("Method without parameters")
06              Console.WriteLine()
07              Console.ReadKey()
08          End Sub 'End of ProcedureExample
09
10          Public Sub ProcedureExample1 (PrintString As String)
11              Console.WriteLine()
12              Console.WriteLine(PrintString)
13              Console.WriteLine()
14              Console.ReadKey()
15          End Sub    'End of ProcedureExample1
16      End Class 'End of ProgramMethod
17
18      Public Class MethodExample
19          Shared Sub Main()
20              ConsoleSetup.SetUpConsole("Procedure Example")
21              Dim pm As New ProgramMethod()
22              pm.ProcedureExample()
23              Dim pm2 As New ProgramMethod()
24              pm2.ProcedureExample1("Method with Parameter")
25          End Sub 'End of Main
26      End Class 'End of MethodExample
27  End Namespace
```

```
M01     Module ConsoleSetup
M02        Sub SetUpConsole(Name As String)
M03            Console.Title = Name
M04            Console.BackgroundColor = ConsoleColor.White
M05            Console.ForegroundColor = ConsoleColor.Black
M06            Console.Clear()
M07        End Sub
M08     End Module
```

Discussion: Procedures Example

As you can see, some of the lines are commented, so no explanation will be given there.

In line 02, Public Class ProgramMethod, the class *ProgramMethod* is specified as Public.

In line 03, Public Sub ProcedureExample(), a Public subroutine called *ProcedureExample* is created. Because there is no parameter specified within the brackets, this subroutine can only work with its own local variables or with global variables, and cannot return a value.

Line 04, Console.WriteLine(), writes an empty line to the console and goes to the start of the next line.

Line 05, Console.WriteLine("Method without parameters"), writes the literal string "Method without parameters" to the console. Remember that *Console* is a class that forms part of the *System Namespace* that was automatically referenced when the program was created.

The following shows the automatic references for this program:

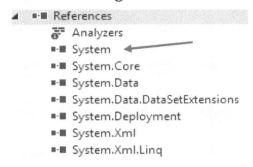

WriteLine() is a method of the *Console Class*.

Do not become confused because we are writing a string to the console. This string is created as a parameter to the *WriteLine* method of the *Console Class*. It has nothing to do with the fact that our subroutine *ProcedureExample* has no parameter specified.

Line 07, Console.ReadKey(), calls the *ReadKey* method of the *Console Class*, and waits for any key to be pressed.

In line 10, Public Sub ProcedureExample1 (PrintString As String), a subroutine *ProcedureExample1* is created, and this time we specify a parameter *PrintString*, as a string type. This means we **must** provide a string type value in the statement where we call this subroutine. In the discussion for line 23 we will look at the calling procedure.

In line 18, Public Class MethodExample, a public class with the name *MethodExample* is created.

Line 19, Shared Sub Main(), creates the compulsory Main() subroutine for the program. This means the *Main()* subroutine of *Class MethodExample*, will be executed first when the program starts.

We'll come back to line 20, ConsoleSetup.SetUpConsole("Procedure Example"), later when we discuss line M02.

In line 21, Dim pm As New ProgramMethod(), we instantiate a new object of the class ProgramMethod, and call it *pm*.

In line 22, pm.ProcedureExample(), we call the *ProcedureExample* method of the instance of class *ProgramMethod* that we created in line 21. We must include the instance name (pm), because, as you will see shortly, we'll end up with another instance of *ProgramMethod*. This time it is called *pm2*, and we must specify which instance we're calling.

In line 23, Dim pm2 As New ProgramMethod(), we do the same as in line 21, but give it the name *pm2*.

In line 24, pm2.ProcedureExample1("Method with Parameter"), we call method *ProcedureExample1* of instance *pm2*. Because *ProcedureExample1* was created with a parameter *PrintString*, we must supply a value for that parameter in our call statement. In this case, we supply a literal value "Method with Parameter".

Discussion: Module ConsoleSetup

Let us look at the *Module ConsoleSetup* from line M01 to M08.

I've added this basic module to the project because we're going to use it to set up the console to display colors that are different from the default colors.

In line M02 we create a subroutine (method) called *SetUpConsole* with a string parameter called *Name*. The value of this variable will be supplied by the calling statement in line 20 of the Namespace ProcedureExample. Please note that this VB Module resides outside of the namespace.

It will be easier to understand what it does if we look at the output, with and without the call to this module.

Output: Procedure Example Without Call

H:\VB Book\Programs\Procedure Example\Procedure Example\bin\Debug\Procedure Example.exe

```
Method without parameters


Method with Parameter

_
```

Output: Procedure Example With Call

```
    Procedure Example


Method without parameters


Method with Parameter

```

Because the first example makes use of the default setting, it uses the complete path of the program as a header, and white text on a black background.

The second example uses the text we supplied in the call parameter as heading, and black text on a white background.

All the output examples, except two, in this book make use of this code in some way or another.

Scope

When using sub procedures and functions we must keep the concept of **scope** in mind. In declaring a variable for instance, we bind the name we give it to that specific instance. Scope refers to the region in the program where that specific name of the variable etc. can be referred to by the rest of the code. Some explanation is in order here.

Program: Scope Example

```
01  Namespace ExplanationOfScope
02      Public Class ScopeExample
03
04          Shared salary As Decimal = 0
05
06          Public Shared Sub Main()
07              SetUpConsole("ExplanationOfScope")
08
```

```vb
09        Console.WriteLine("Initial Salary of Class = {0}", salary)
10        Console.ReadKey()
11
12        Test1()
13        Console.WriteLine("Salary of Class after Test1 = {0}", salary)
14        Console.ReadKey()
15
16        Test2(salary)
17        Console.WriteLine("Salary of Class after Test2 = {0}", salary)
18        Console.ReadKey()
19
20    End Sub
21
22    Shared Sub Test1()
23        salary = CDec(100.99)
24    End Sub
25
26    Shared Sub Test2(sal As Decimal)
27        Dim salary As Decimal
28        salary = sal * 2
29    End Sub

30    Shared Sub SetUpConsole(Name)
31        Console.Title = Name
32        Console.BackgroundColor = ConsoleColor.White
33        Console.ForegroundColor = ConsoleColor.Black
34        Console.Clear()
35    End Sub
36  End Class
37 End Namespace
```

Discussion: Scope Example

The lines of code have again been numbered, to make explanation easier.

In line 4, Shared salary As Decimal = 0, we declared a variable called *salary* of the type *decimal*, and initiated it to the value zero. As you can see this variable is declared in the class, and because we used Shared instead of Dim, it will be available to all the code in the class. Such a variable is a global variable.

In line 9, Console.WriteLine("Initial Salary of Class = {0}", salary), we use a place holder in the string to write the value of the variable *salary* to the console. As you can see in the output, the value is 0.

In line 12, Test1(), we call the method *Test1* without a parameter.

In line 13, Console.WriteLine("Salary of Class after Test1 = {0}", salary), we use a place holder again to write the value of the variable *salary* to the console. As you can see from the output, the value of the variable that has been declared in the class has been changed. Obviously because its declaration is global.

In line 16, Test2(salary), we call the method *Test2* with a parameter which contains the class variable *salary*. The parameter in the declaration of the method *Test2* (statement 26, Shared Sub Test2(sal As Decimal)), is called *sal*, and contains the value of the class variable *salary*, which is still 100.99.

In line 17, Console.WriteLine("Salary of Class after Test2 = {0}", salary), we again write the value of *salary* to the console.

In line 22, Shared Sub Test1(), we declare a *shared* subroutine without a parameter and call it *Test1*.

In line 23, salary = CDec(100.99), we changed the value of the variable *salary* to 100.99. The compiler sees the value 100.99 as type *double* which is not compatible with type *decimal*, and will raise an error during compilation. Therefore, we use the statement CDec(100.99) to change (cast) the type to decimal.

In line 26, Shared Sub **Test2(sal** As Decimal), we declare a *shared* subroutine with the decimal parameter called *sal*.

In line 27, Dim salary As Decimal, we use the Dim statement to declare a variable with the same name as the class variable, i.e. *salary*.

In line 28, salary = sal * 2, we multiply the value of *sal* (which refers to the class variable *salary*) by 2 and assign the value to *salary*. In other words, the value of *salary* is now 201.98.

Output: Scope Example

```
ExplanationOfScope
Initial Salary of Class = 0
Salary of Class after Test1 = 100.99
Salary of Class after Test2 = 100.99
```

What is going on? The value written in line 17 is the same as the value written in line 13. Shouldn't it be 201.98? That is after all, the value of salary after we called *Test2*.

No, the value is correct! This is where the scope comes in. Because we declared the variable *salary* inside the method *Test2*, it is local to *Test2*. In other words, it isn't the same variable that we declared in the class, even if the name is the same. Because the variable declared in the class is global, line 4 refers to that variable, instead of the local variable declared in statement 27.

So, how can we rectify this? Obviously, there are a number of ways to do this, but we're going to use a *function* here.

We can change *Test2* to a function with the following code:

```
01      Shared Function Test2(Sal As Decimal) As Decimal
02          Dim salary As Decimal
03          salary = Sal * 2
04          Return salary
05      End Function
```

A function returns a value, while a sub procedure doesn't. In statement 01, Shared Function Test2(Sal As Decimal) As Decimal, we declare a *function Test2* of the type *decimal*. Because it is declared as decimal, we must make sure that the value we return must also be of the same type. In the example it is the case.

In statement 04, Return salary, we use the keyword Return to accomplish that.

Because we're returning a value, we must change the call statement in Sub Main() to be an assignment. The code is changed as follows: salary = Test2(salary). Just remember that the type of the variable, to the left of the assign statement (=), must be of the same type as the function, or else an error will be generated.

Output: Produced After Changes:

```
      ExplanationOfScope

Initial Salary of Class = 0
Salary of Class after Test1 = 100.99
Salary of Class after Test2 = 201.98
```

Which is what we expected.

CHAPTER 5

CONTROL STRUCTURES

Just as we use certain sentences in normal language to give instructions, we do the same in a programming language. We call those instructions, statements.

OK. The statements we need to write to accomplish the required action falls into three categories: sequence, selection and iteration.

By putting together the statements in a combination of these three categories, we can write any program.

SEQUENCE

Sequence is easy. One statement following another from start to finish.

Diagram of Sequential Statements

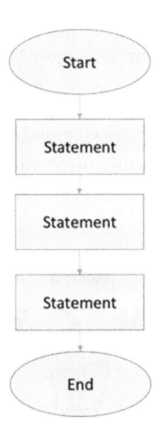

Program: Sequence Example

```
Namespace Sequence
    Class Test 'Class declaration
        Shared x As Integer 'Variable declaration

        Shared Sub Main() 'Method declaration

            x = 12 * 30        'Statement 1

            Console.WriteLine(x) 'Statement 2
            Console.ReadKey()    'Statement 3
        End Sub
    End Class
End Namespace
```

In this example the number 360 (12 x 30) will be displayed on the screen (the console).

Fine, but not very helpful. If you want to do a single thing that's fine, but not very helpful if you want to choose between things, or keep on doing the same thing for a while, and then stop.

SELECTION

To choose between options we use selection. Basically, something like, "if it rains, take an umbrella, if not just leave". Normally we do that by checking the truth of the condition. If it rains, then the condition is true and we take the umbrella.

Diagram of Selection Statements

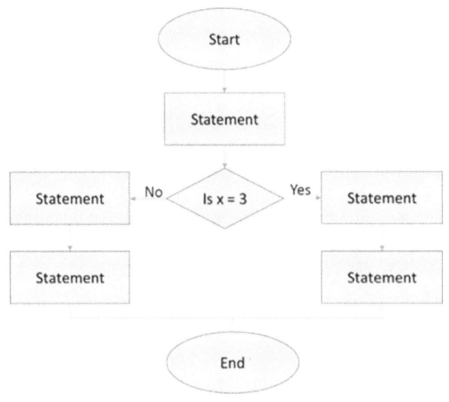

Generic Syntax of the If Statement

Multiline syntax:

If condition [Then]
  [statements]
[ElseIf elseifcondition [Then]
  [elseifstatements]]
[Else
  [elsestatements]]
End If

Single-line syntax:

If condition Then [statements] [Else [elsestatements]]

Note

When this notation is used in this book, the part between square brackets []
is conditional. It can be included if necessary or left out if not. The part
between the curly brackets separated by the pipe signal |, means that one of
the indicated statements must be included.

Discussion of the parts of each statement.

Condition is required. This is an Expression. It must evaluate to True or
False, or to a data type that is implicitly convertible to Boolean. If the
expression is a Nullable Boolean variable that evaluates to Nothing, the
condition is treated as if the expression is False and the Else block is
executed.

Then is required in the single-line syntax, but optional in the multiline
syntax.

Statements are optional. It consists of one or more statements following the
If...Then and are executed if the condition evaluates to True.

Elseif is a condition and is required if ElseIf is present. This expression must evaluate to True or False, or to a data type that is implicitly convertible to Boolean.

Elseif statements are optional, and consists of one or more statements following ElseIf...Then. These are executed if the elseif condition evaluates to True.

Else statements are optional and consist of one or more statements that are executed if no previous condition exists or the elseif condition expression evaluates to True.

End If terminates the multiline version of the If...Then...Else block.

Program: Selection Example

```
Namespace Selection
  Class Program
    Shared Sub Main()
      Dim conString As String
      Dim firstVal As Integer
      Dim secondVal As Integer

      SetUpConsole("Selection")

      conString = Console.ReadLine()
      firstVal = Convert.ToInt16(ConString)
      conString = Console.ReadLine()
      secondVal = Convert.ToInt16(ConString)

      If firstVal = secondVal Then
        conString = "Numbers are equal"
      Else
        conString = "Numbers are not equal"
      End If
```

```
        Console.WriteLine(conString)
        Console.ReadKey()
    End Sub

    Shared Sub SetUpConsole(name As String)
        Console.Title = name
        Console.BackgroundColor = ConsoleColor.White
        Console.ForegroundColor = ConsoleColor.Black
        Console.Clear()
    End Sub
  End Class
End Namespace
```

Output: Selection Example

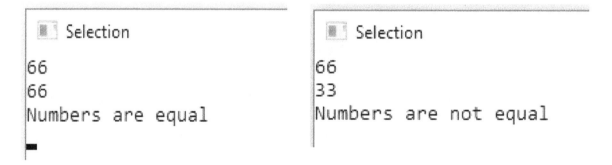

Let's look at the code. We'll only look at the applicable code and code not seen previously.

In the following *DIM* statements

    Dim conString As String

    Dim firstVal As Integer

    Dim secondVal As Integer

We declared one *string type* and two *integer type* variables. Nothing strange, but important to note.

If we assign a value to a variable of a different type, an error will be generated, even if the value is comparable to what the receiving variable can handle.

In the statement, conString = Console.ReadLine(), we read a value from the console and stored it in the string variable *conString*. The value that we read in our example is 66. Well, 66 is an integer, so in theory we can assign it to the integer variable *firstVal*. Unfortunately, it doesn't work that way. The one variable was still declared as string and the other as integer, thus they are not compatible. In the assign statement we must convert the string variable to an integer value. This is accomplished by the ToInt16 Method of the *Convert Class*, as in the statement firstVal = Convert.ToInt16(conString).

There is another selection statement, called the *Case* statement and we'll look at it later.

ITERATION

The third option is to repeat something until we want to stop. That is called iteration. To accomplish that, we want to repeat some action, or a sequence of actions, while the condition is true, or until it becomes false, for a number of times, or once for each element in a collection. These iterations are called loops. There are a few of these loop statements, namely Do While, Do Until, the For loop that iterates for a predetermined number of times, and the For Each loop that iterates through each element in a collection.

Diagram of Iteration

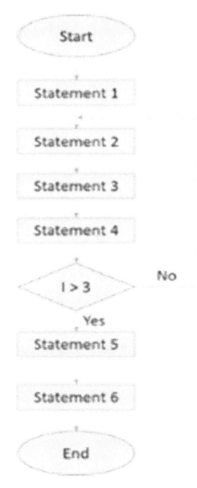

Program: Example of a DO WHILE Loop

```
01 Namespace DoLoop
02   Class Doloop
03     Shared Sub Main()
04       Dim conString As String = "Enter an integer per line" & vbCrLf
05       Dim firstVal As Integer
06       Dim secondVal As Integer
07
08       SetUpConsole("Do Loop Example")
09
10       Console.WriteLine(conString)
11
12       Do
13          conString = Console.ReadLine()
14
15          firstVal = Convert.ToInt16(conString)
16
17          conString = Console.ReadLine()
18
19          secondVal = Convert.ToInt16(conString)
20
21          If (firstVal = secondVal) Then
22              conString = "Numbers are equal" & vbCrLf
23
24          Else
25              conString = "Numbers are not equal" & vbCrLf
26
27          End If
28
29          Console.WriteLine(conString)
30
31          conString = "Press n and enter to stop, enter to continue"
32
```

```
33          Console.WriteLine(conString)
34
35          conString = Console.ReadLine
36       Loop While (conString <> "n")
37
38    End Sub
39
40    Shared Sub SetUpConsole(name)
41          Console.Title = name
42          Console.BackgroundColor = ConsoleColor.White
43          Console.ForegroundColor = ConsoleColor.Black
44          Console.Clear()
45     End Sub
46   End Class
47 End Namespace
```

Output: Do Loop Example

```
Do Loop Example
Enter an integer per line

66
33
Numbers are not equal

Press n and enter to stop, enter to continue

66
66
Numbers are equal

Press n and enter to stop, enter to continue
n
```

Discussion: Do Loop Example

Let's look at the code. We'll only look at the applicable code and code not seen previously.

Remember that, as in previous examples, the lines of code have been numbered to make discussion easier.

In line 04, Dim conString As String = "Enter an integer per line" & vbCrLf, we set up the variable *conString,* to use as a parameter when we write to the console. As part of the same line we see & and *vbCrLf.* In this case the ampersand (&) is used to concatenate, (add) whatever follows to the string. Obviously, this is not a numeric add, but is used to build a string. Here we concatenate the VB constant *vbCrLf* to the string value. The *Cr* stands for carriage return, and the *Lf* for line feed. In essence this forces the next output to the first character of the next line.

In line 12, Do, we start the *Do Loop* with the *Do* statement.

The loop is ended in line 36, Loop While (conString <> "n"), with the *Loop While* statement.

Because the *Do* statement occurs first without any indication of the value to test against, it is obvious that all the statements that follows, up to the *Loop While* statement, will be executed at least once. The condition is included in the *Loop While* statement. In this case (conString <> "n"). If the string is less than (<), or greater than (>) the letter "n", the loop is executed again, starting from the *Do* statement.

Different Do Loops: a Quick Peek

While/Until

Do { While | Until } condition
   [statements]
   [Continue Do]
   [statements]
   [Exit Do]
   [statements]
Loop

Or,

Do
   [statements]
   [Continue Do]
   [statements]
   [Exit Do]
   [statements]
Loop { While | Until } condition

In this notation the part between square brackets [] is conditional. It can be included if necessary or left out if not. The part between the curly brackets separated by the pipe signal |, means that one of the indicated statements must be included.

The parts of a Do Loop

Do is required. Starts the definition of the Do loop.

While is required unless Until is used. Repeat the loop until condition is False.

Until is required unless While is used. Repeat the loop until condition is True.

Condition is optional. This is a *Boolean* expression. If the condition is "Nothing", Visual Basic treats it as *False*.

Statements are optional. One or more statements that are repeated while, or until the condition is *True*.

Continue Do is optional. This transfers control to the next iteration of the *Do loop*.

Exit Do is optional. This transfers control out of the *Do loop*.

Loop is required. Terminates the definition of the Do loop.

The For Loop

Let's look at the generic syntax of a For loop:

For counter [As datatype] = start To end [Step]
   [statements]
   [Continue For]
   [statements]
   [Exit For]
   [statements]
Next [counter]

In this notation the part between square brackets [] is conditional. It can be included if necessary or left out if not. The part between the curly brackets separated by the pipe signal |, means that one of the indicated statements must be included.

Counter is required in the *For* statement. Counter is a *Numeric* variable and is the control variable for the loop.

Datatype is optional and is the data type of counter variable.

Start is required and must be a numeric expression. It is the initial value of the counter.

End is required and must be a numeric expression. It is the final value of the counter.

Step is optional and must be a numeric expression. It is the amount by which the counter is incremented each time through the loop.

Statements are optional. It is one or more statements between For and Next that run the specified number of times.

Continue For is optional and transfers control to the next loop iteration before the Next statement is reached.

Exit For is optional and transfers control out of the *For loop*.

Next is required and terminates the definition of the For loop.

Program: The For Loop Example

```vbnet
01  Namespace ForLoop
02    Class ForLoop
03      Shared Sub Main()
04        Dim i As Integer
05
06        SetUpConsole("For Loop Example")
07
08        For i = 1 To 10
09          Console.Write(i & ",")
10        Next
11        Console.WriteLine()
12
13        For i = 1 To 10 Step 2
14          Console.Write(i & ",")
15        Next
16        Console.WriteLine()
17
18        For i = 10 To 1 Step -1
19          Console.Write(i & ",")
20        Next
21        Console.WriteLine()
22
23        Dim min As Integer = 1
24        Dim max As Integer = 10
25
26        For i = min To max
27          If i < max Then
28            Console.Write(i & ",")
29          Else
30            Console.WriteLine(i)
31          End If
32        Next
```

```
33        Console.ReadKey()
34     End Sub
35
36     Shared Sub SetUpConsole(Name As String)
37        Console.Title = Name
38        Console.BackgroundColor = ConsoleColor.White
39        Console.ForegroundColor = ConsoleColor.Black
40        Console.Clear()
41     End Sub
42   End Class
43 End Namespace
```

Output: The For Loop Example

```
For Loop Example
1,2,3,4,5,6,7,8,9,10,
1,3,5,7,9,
10,9,8,7,6,5,4,3,2,1,
1,2,3,4,5,6,7,8,9,10
```

Discussion: For Loop Example

The first For Loop starts in line 8, For i = 1 To 10, and uses the counter i, with literal values 1 to 10, for the number of iterations. Because the optional *Step* statement is not supplied, a step of one is inferred. The loop is ended in line 10, Next. The *Next* statement increments the counter by one and passes control back to the *For* statement in line 8.

The parameter for the statement in line 9, Console.Write(i & ","), uses the current value of *i*, and concatenates a comma to the string to be written. Note that it leaves a comma with nothing following at the end of the printed line. We will rectify that with an If statement in a later example of a For loop.

The For loop starting in line 13, For i = 1 To 10 Step 2, uses the *Step* statement of 2, and thus ads 2 to the counter at the end of each iteration.

The For loop starting on line 18, For i = 10 To 1 Step -1, uses a *Step* of -1 and will subtract 1 from the counter with each iteration. The counter specified should obviously start with a value greater than the end value for the loop to execute.

In lines 23, Dim min As Integer = 1, and 24, Dim max As Integer = 10, we declare the variables *min* and *max* and initiate it with the start and end values for the counter.

The For declaration in line 26, For i = min To max, uses the variables as starting and ending values for the counter.

As promised, the if statement starting in line 27, If i < max Then, and ending in line 31, End If, checks to see if the loop has reached its end, and if it has then it doesn't concatenate the comma to the string. It looks much better without the wayward comma at the end.

There is another type of For loop called a "For Each" loop, but we'll look at that later.

Interesting

The 1944 IBM Mark I Computer measured 51 feet long, 8 feet tall, and 8 feet deep. It had more than 750,000 parts, used 530 miles of wire, and weighed more than 5 tons. A four-horsepower **electric motor** and drive shaft drove all the mechanical parts by a system of interlocking gears, counters, switches, and control circuits. Input was entered by punching holes in paper tape that was then fed into the machine. Output was handled automatically by electric typewriters.

Interesting – Grace Murray Hopper

 In 1952 she had an operational compiler. "Nobody believed that," she said. "I had a running compiler and nobody would touch it. They told me computers could only do arithmetic."

Admiral Hopper is also called the "Mother" of COBOL, which she was working on in 1955.

On the building of bigger computers: "In pioneer days they used oxen for heavy pulling, and when one ox couldn't budge a log, they didn't try to grow a larger ox. We shouldn't be trying for bigger computers, but for more systems of computers."

On change: "Humans are allergic to change. They love to say, 'We've always done it this way.' I try to fight that. That's why I have a clock on my wall that runs counter-clockwise."

On calculating the value of information: "A business' accounts receivable file is much more important than its accounts payable file."

On information and knowledge: "We're flooding people with information. We need to feed it through a processor. A human must turn information into intelligence or knowledge. We've tended to forget that no computer will ever ask a new question."

On advice to the young (whom she defines as "anybody half my age"): "You manage things, you lead people. We went overboard on management and forgot about leadership. It might help if we ran the MBAs out of Washington."

CHAPTER 6

STORING AND RETRIEVING DATA

It is all good and well to be able to enter and display data using the console, but not very useful if it all disappears when you switch off the computer or close the program. There must be a way to store the data more permanently and access it as needed.

The main storage process makes use of a database, where data are stored in the form of tables where each table represents a file, and each column represents a data field. Each row will then represent a record. A table will be something like all of the employee records. A record will be the data for a specific employee, and the data field an item like, name, ID etc. There are many different types of database systems, like Oracle, SQL Server and Microsoft Access. To handle these databases, we have to use another language called SQL (Structured Query Language) which is a general programming language to manipulate relational databases.

As this is only an introduction to VB programming, we will leave the database systems and concentrate on something that is available in VB, namely files.

Database Example

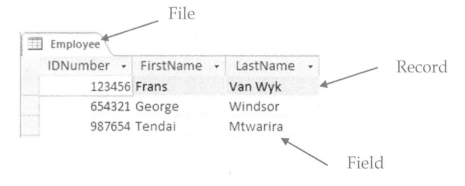

File Example

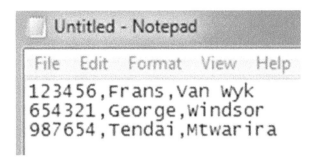

FILE HANDLING

A file can be seen as a collection of records about something like, for instance, employees. Each line in the file will represent a record, and the contents of the record will be the different fields as stated for databases. In this case, we store the fields for a certain employee on one line in the file. Obviously one big string of data means nothing if we have no means to distinguish one piece of data from the next. A string looking like this:

"Frans Van Wyk480706509208612 ConnorAvenueWestdeneBloemfonteinSouth Africa9301"

doesn't mean much if you don't know me, and even then, you cannot possibly know all the employees intimately. The only way we will be able to make sense of a record is if we know where one field ends, and another starts. We can rectify this problem by using a delimiter to separate the fields. For a text file, we usually use the comma. The string as above will then look something like this:

"Frans Van Wyk,4807065092086,12 Connor Avenue,Westdene, Bloemfontein,South Africa,9301"

Now it's much easier to make sense of the different fields.

Program: File Handling Example

This program writes to a file called test.txt that resides in the root directory of the D: drive. It writes one line, reads the data from that file and displays it on the console. It then writes another line to the same file, but adds it at the end of the file (appends the file). It then reads all the data from the file and displays it on the console.

```
01  imports System.IO 'Needed for StreamReader and StreamWriter
02
03  Namespace FileHandlingExample
04    Class Program
05      Shared Sub Main()
06        Dim lines As String = "Hi there, my dear old friend" & vbCrLf
07        Dim file As StreamWriter
08        SetUpConsole("File Handling Example")
09        file = My.Computer.FileSystem.OpenTextFileWriter("D:/test.txt",
10                                                          False)
11        file.WriteLine(lines)
12        file.Close()
13
14        Dim fileReader As StreamReader
15
16        fileReader=My.Computer.FileSystem.OpenTextFileReader(
17                                              "D:/test.txt")
18
19        Dim text As String = fileReader.ReadToEnd()
20
21        fileReader.Close()
22
23        Console.WriteLine(text)
24
25        Using file1 As New StreamWriter("D:/test.txt", True)
26          file1.WriteLine("How are you?")
27        End Using
```

```
28
29        Dim text1 As String
30
31        Using fileReader1 As New StreamReader("D:/test.txt")
32           text1 = fileReader1.ReadToEnd()
33        End Using
34
35        Console.WriteLine(text1)
36        Console.ReadKey()
37     End Sub
38
39     Shared Sub SetUpConsole(Name As String)
40        Console.Title = Name
41        Console.BackgroundColor = ConsoleColor.White
42        Console.ForegroundColor = ConsoleColor.Black
43        Console.Clear()
44     End Sub
45   End Class
46 End Namespace
```

Remember anything that appears after a single quote character (') is seen as remarks and ignored by the compiler.

Output: File Handling Example

```
File Handling Example

Hi there, my dear old friend


Hi there, my dear old friend

How are you?

_
```

Discussion: File Handling Example

In line 1, imports System.IO, we import the *System.IO* Namespace to be able to access the classes we'll need to do file handling.

In line 6, Dim lines As String = "Hi there, my dear old friend" & vbCrLf, we declare and populate the string with a literal value and concatenate the VB constant vbCrLf to the literal value. Nothing new here.

In line 7, Dim file As StreamWriter, we create a *streamwriter* object called *file*. The *streamwriter* class forms part of the *System.IO* namespace that we imported in line 1. (See page 217.)

My.Computer.FileSystem.OpenTextFileWriter("D:/test.txt", False), in lines 9 and 10, assigns a *textfilewriter* to our *streamwriter* declared in line 7 as *file*. This statement uses the current computer's file system and opens a channel to a file called *test.txt* on the *D: drive*. We added the Boolean value *False* to specify that any file by the same name in the same directory will be overwritten.

In line 11, file.WriteLine(lines), we use the *file* object to write the contents of the variable *lines* to the channel we created in line 6.

In line 12, file.Close(), we close the *file* channel to flush its contents to the disk to create the file *D:/test.txt* and close the channel.

In line 14, Dim fileReader As StreamReader, we create a *streamreader* object called *fileReader*. The *streamreader* class also forms part of the *System.IO* namespace that we imported in line 1. (See page 217.)

fileReader=My.Computer.FileSystem.OpenTextFileReader("D:/test.txt"), in lines 16 and 17, creates a *streamreader* object called *filereader*. This statement uses the current computer's file system and opens a channel to a file called *test.txt* on the *D: drive*. If the file does not exist an error will be generated, but we'll look at that in the Calling External Programs section.

In line 19, Dim text As String = fileReader.ReadToEnd(), we created a variable called *text*, and assigned the value returned by the function *fileReader.ReadToEnd()*, to it. This function forms part of the streamreader class and reads everything in the file specified. *D:/test.txt* in this case.

In line 21, fileReader.Close(), we close the channel to the file used in line 19.

In line 23, Console.WriteLine(text), we write the value of the variable *text* to the console.

In line 25, Using file1 As New StreamWriter("D:/test.txt", True), we create a block of text with the *using* statement. It creates a new instance of *streamwriter* called *file1*, and opens the channel to the file *D:/test.txt*. We added the *true* statement to append the text to the end of the file. Remember the *false* statement in line 10 forced the deletion of the file. For the *Using* statement definition see page 219.

In line 26, file1.WriteLine("How are you?"), we use the *WriteLine* statement to add the literal value "How are you?" to the end of the file we connected to the channel in line 25.

In line 27, End Using, we close the block of code we started in line 25. You will notice that we didn't close the streamwriter as we did in line 12. It is not necessary because the *end using* statement disposes all the resources we used in the using block.

In line 29, Dim text1 As String, we create a string variable called *text1* to receive the contents we read from the file.

In line 31, Using fileReader1 As New StreamReader("D:/test.txt"), we create a using block that connects a new *streamreader* called *fileReader1* to the file on disk.

In line 32, text1 = fileReader1.ReadToEnd(), we read the whole contents of the file connected to *fileReader1* and assign it to the string variable *text1*.

In line 33, End Using, we end the *using* block and thus dispose of all the resources we used in that block.

The rest of the code is familiar, and we're not going to discuss that.

CHAPTER 7

OPERATORS

An operator is a piece of code that performs an operation on another piece of code that contains a value. This can be things such as variables, constants, literals and properties.

Arithmetic Operators

These operators perform familiar arithmetic operations like add, subtract, multiply etc.

OPERATOR	PURPOSE	EXAMPLE	RESULT
^	Exponentiation	2 ^ 3	(2 * 2 * 2) = 8 .
-	Negation	- 2	- 2
*	Multiplication	2 * 3	6
/	Division	3 / 2	1.5
\	Integer division	17\5	3
Mod	Modulus	17 Mod 5	2
+	Addition	2 + 3	5
-	Subtraction	3 - 2	1

Comparison Operators

These operators are used to compare two expressions and returns a value of either true or false, depending on the outcome of the comparison.

OPERATOR	PURPOSE	EXAMPLE	RESULT
=	Equals	A = B	True if A equals B
<>	Not equals	A <> B	True if A does not equal B
<	Less than	A < B	True if A is less than B
< =	Less than or equal to	A < = B	True if A is less than or equal to B
>	Greater than	A > B	True if A is greater than B
> =	Greater than or equal to	A > = B	True if A is greater than or equal to B
Is	Equality of two objects	emp Is mgr	True if emp and mgr refer to the same object
IsNot	Inequality of two objects	emp IsNot mgr	True if emp and mgr refer to different objects
TypeOf...Is ...	Object is of a certain type	TypeOf obj Is Manager	True if obj points to a Manager object
Like	Matches a text pattern	value Like " ### - #### "	True if value contains three digits, a dash, and four digits

The list on the next page lists characters that have special meanings to the Like operator.

CHARACTER(S)	MEANING
?	Matches any single character
*	Matches any zero or more characters
#	Matches any single digit
[characters]	Matches any of the characters between the brackets
[!characters]	Matches any character not between the brackets
A - Z	When inside brackets, matches any character in the range A to Z

Logical Operators

These operators allow us to evaluate one or more expressions and return a Boolean value depending on the outcome.

OPERATOR	PURPOSE	EXAMPLE	RESULT
Not	Logical or bitwise negation	Not A	True if A is false
And	Logical or bitwise And	A And B	True if A and B are both true
Or	Logical or bitwise Or	A Or B	True if A or B or Both are True
Xor but	Logical or bitwise Exclusive Or	A Xor B	True if A or B not both are true
AndAlso	Logical or bitwise And with Short-circuit evaluation	A AndAlso B	True if A and B are both true
OrElse	Logical or bitwise Or with Short-circuit evaluation	A OrElse B	True if A or B or both are true

Operator Precedence

The following table lists the operators in order of precedence. When evaluating an expression, the program evaluates an operator before it evaluates those lower than it in the list. When operators are on the same line, the program evaluates them from left to right.

OPERATOR	DESCRIPTION
^	Exponentiation
-	Negation
* , /	Multiplication and division
\	Integer division
Mod	Modulus
+ , - , +	Addition, subtraction and concatenation
&	Concatenation
<< , >>	Bit shift
= , <> , < , <= , > , >= , Like, Is, Isnot, TypeOf … Is …	All comparisons
Not	Logical and bitwise negation
And , AndAlso	Logical and bitwise And with and without Short-circuit evaluation
Xor , Or , OrElse	Logical and bitwise Xor, and Or with and Without Short-circuit evaluation

Comparison Operators

These operators are used to compare two expressions and returns a value of either true or false, depending on the outcome of the comparison.

OPERATOR	PURPOSE	EXAMPLE	RESULT
= =	Equals	A = = B	True if A equals B
!=	Not equals	A !=B	True if A does not equal B
<	Less than	A < B	True if A is less than B
< =	Less than or equal to	A < = B	True if A is less than or equal to B
>	Greater than	A > B	True if A is greater than B
> =	Greater than or equal to	A > = B	True if A is greater than or equal to B
Is	Equality of two objects	emp Is mgr	True if emp and mgr refer to the same object
IsNot	Inequality of two objects	emp IsNot mgr	True if emp and mgr refer to different objects
TypeOf...Is ...	Object is of a certain type	TypeOf obj Is Manager	True if obj points to a Manager object

Logical Operators

These operators allow us to evaluate one or more expressions and return a Boolean value depending on the outcome.

OPERATOR	PURPOSE	EXAMPLE	RESULT
!	Logical or bitwise negation	! A	True if A is false
&	Logical or bitwise And	A & B	True if A and B are both true
|	Logical or bitwise Or	A | B	True if A or B or

			Both are True
^	Logical or bitwise Exclusive Or	A ^ B	True if A or B but not both are true
&&	Logical or bitwise And with Short-circuit evaluation	A && B	True if A and B are both true
| |	Logical or bitwise Or with Short-circuit evaluation	A | | B	True if A or B or both are true

Operator Precedence

The following table lists the operators in order of precedence. When evaluating an expression, the program evaluates an operator before it evaluates those lower than it in the list. When operators are on the same line, the program evaluates them from left to right.

OPERATOR	DESCRIPTION
-	Negation
* , /	Multiplication and division
%	Modulus
+ , - , +	Addition, subtraction and concatenation
+	Concatenation
<< , >>	Bit shift
= , <> , < , <= , > , >= Is, Isnot, TypeOf … Is …	All comparisons
!	Logical and bitwise negation
&, &&	Logical and bitwise And with and without Short-circuit evaluation
^ , | , | |	Logical and bitwise Xor, and Or with and Without Short-circuit evaluation

Assignment Operators

These are operators that are used to assign a value to the operand to the left of the operator.

OPERATOR	EXAMPLE	ORIGINAL SYNTAX EQUIVALENT
=	A = B	A = B
^=	A ^= B	A = A ^ B
*=	A *= B	A = A * B
/=	A /= B	A = A / B
\=	A \= B	A = A \ B
+ =	A + = B	A = A + B
- =	A - = B	A = A - B
& =	A & = B	A = A & B
< < =	A < < = B	A = A < < B
> > =	A > > = B	A = A > > B

There are no assignment operators corresponding to Mod or the Boolean operators.

Programming Quotes

- The best thing about a boolean is even if you are wrong, you are only off by a bit. (Anonymous)
- Without requirements or design, programming is the art of adding bugs to an empty text file. (Louis Srygley)
- Before software can be reusable it first has to be usable. (Ralph Johnson)
- If builders built buildings the way programmers wrote programs, then the first woodpecker that came along would destroy civilization. (Gerald Weinberg)
- There are two ways to write error-free programs; only the third one works. (Alan J. Perlis)
- One man's crappy software is another man's full-time job. (Jessica Gaston)
- A good programmer is someone who always looks both ways before crossing a one-way street. (Doug Linder)
- Always code as if the guy who ends up maintaining your code will be a violent psychopath who knows where you live. (Martin Golding)
- Walking on water and developing software from a specification are easy if both are frozen. (Edward V Berard)
- If debugging is the process of removing software bugs, then programming must be the process of putting them in. (Edsger Dijkstra)
- Software undergoes beta testing shortly before it's released. Beta is Latin for "still doesn't work". (Anonymous)
- Programming today is a race between software engineers striving to build bigger and better idiot-proof programs, and the universe trying to produce bigger and better idiots. So far, the universe is winning. (Rick Cook)
- There are only two kinds of programming languages: those people always bitch about and those nobody uses. (Bjarne Stroustrup)

CHAPTER 8

ARRAYS

The best way to explain the concept of arrays is by doing an example.

By now you should be familiar with declaring normal variables of different types.

If we want to use three names, then we can declare three String variables.

```
Dim name1 As String
Dim name2 As String
Dim name3 As String
```

Or we can shorten this by doing it on one line:

```
Dim name1, name2, name3 As String
```

Then we can store a value in each of the three variables.

```
name1 = "John"
name2 = "Paul"
name3 = "Mary"
```

Or if we wanted to shorten the whole lot a bit, we could declare the variable and assign a value in one go.

```
Dim name1 As String = "John"
Dim name2 As String = "Paul"
Dim name3 As String = "Mary"
```

Just remember that we cannot use Dim name1, name2, name3 As String, and assign values at the same time.

If we now want to display the names, we can say:

```
Console.WriteLine(name1)
Console.WriteLine(name2)
Console.WriteLine(name3)
```

That doesn't look like too much work, but what if we want to do the same for 50 or 100 names? Then it becomes quite a drag.

What if we want to type in 50 names from the keyboard and use them for some action? Then it's even worse. If we want to enter names but don't know beforehand how many there will be, it becomes a nightmare. There surely must be an easier way.

That's where the concept of arrays comes into its own.

An array (sometimes called a matrix or a table) consists of a number of variables with the same name, where each is identified by its position in a sequence of values. The first, second, third, etc. This position is identified by an index of the type Integer.

A one-dimensional array consists of a number of rows each containing a value of the same type.

Names

0.	Peter
1.	Paul
2.	Mary

Something very important to note here is that the position starts at 0 and not at 1. As we said, the position in the array is identified by an index of the type Integer.

Let's declare an array called names that consists of five segments.

Dim names(4) As String. The 4 represents the upper-bound of the array index. In this case there will be five segments: 0,1,2,3 and 4.

I'll be explaining this further at the hand of the following example program. The rows are again numbered for the sake of clarity.

Program: Arrays Example

```
01 Namespace Arrays
02
03   Class Arrays
04     Shared aNames() As String = {"Peter", "Paul", "Mary", "Margie",
05                                                "John"}
06
07     Shared Sub Main()
08
09       SetUpConsole("Arrays Example")
10
11       Arr()
12       NoArr()
13
14     End Sub
15
16     Shared Sub Arr()
17
18       Dim index As Integer
19
20       For index = 0 To 4
21          Console.Write((index + 1) & ". ")
22          Console.WriteLine(aNames(index))
23       Next
24       Console.WriteLine()
25
26       Dim names1 = {"Peter", "Paul", "Mary", "Margie", "John"}
27
28       For Each name In names1
```

```
29          Console.WriteLine(name)
30      Next
31      Console.WriteLine()
32      Console.WriteLine("Press Enter to continue")
33
34      Console.ReadKey()
35
36   End Sub
37
38   Shared Sub NoArr()
39      Dim name1 As String
40      Dim name2 As String
41      Dim name3 As String
42      Dim name4 As String
43      Dim name5 As String
44
45      'Dim name1, name2, name3, name4, name5 As String
46
47      name1 = "Peter"
48      name2 = "Paul"
49      name3 = "Mary"
50      name4 = "Margie"
51      name5 = "John"
52
53      Console.WriteLine()
54
55      Console.WriteLine("1. " & name1)
56      Console.WriteLine("2. " & name2)
57      Console.WriteLine("3. " & name3)
58      Console.WriteLine("4. " & name4)
59      Console.WriteLine("5. " & name5)
60      Console.WriteLine()
61
62      Console.WriteLine(name1)
```

```
63        Console.WriteLine(name2)
64        Console.WriteLine(name3)
65        Console.WriteLine(name4)
66        Console.WriteLine(name5)
67
68        Console.ReadKey()
69
70    End Sub
71    Shared Sub SetUpConsole(Name As String)
72        Console.Title = Name
73        Console.BackgroundColor = ConsoleColor.White
74        Console.ForegroundColor = ConsoleColor.Black
75        Console.Clear()
76    End Sub
77  End Class
78 End Namespace
```

Output: Arrays Example

Output 1 (Arr())

Arrays Example

```
1. Peter
2. Paul
3. Mary
4. Margie
5. John

Peter
Paul
Mary
Margie
John

Press Enter to continue
```

Output 2 (NoArr())

```
1. Peter
2. Paul
3. Mary
4. Margie
5. John

Peter
Paul
Mary
Margie
John
```

Discussion: Arrays Example

In lines 4 and 5 we declared an array called *aNames* as string and assigned values to the five segments. We have not given it an upper-bound index because the number of values assigned does that automatically. We have declared it as *Shared*, so we can use it anywhere in the Class. Remember that we could have done the whole statement in one line, but we split it over two lines for the sake of clarity.

In line 11 we call a subroutine called *Arr()* with an empty parameter.

In line 12 we call a subroutine called *NoArr()* with an empty parameter.

Line 16, Shared Sub Arr(), declares the subroutine Arr().

In line 20, For index = 0 To 4, we start a For loop to repeat five times.

Line 21, Console.Write((index + 1) & ". "), writes the number of index+1 (remember the index starts at 0 but we want to number the names starting with 1), and concatenates a period followed by a space to the string to be written to the Console.

In line 22, Console.WriteLine(aNames(index)), we write the segment of the array *aNames* indicated by the index. It is important to note that we're using the array declared and populated in the class (lines 4 and 5).

In line 26, Dim names1 = {"Peter", "Paul", "Mary", "Margie", "John"}, we declare an array called *names1*. Note that we didn't specify the number of segments or the data type. The number of segments is inferred from the number of values we assign to the array, and the data type is inferred from the data type of the values assigned.

In line 28, For Each name In names1, we use a *For Each* loop to write all the names in the array *names1*. Take note that we don't have to declare *name*. It automatically assumes the data type of the array. *Names1* in this case.

In line 38, Shared Sub NoArr(), we declare the subroutine *NoArr()*. Where the subroutine *Arr()* used arrays, this subroutine does not.

In lines 39 to 43 we declare variables of the data type String to receive the name values. We could use the declaration shown commented out in line 45,

'Dim name1, name2, name3, name4, name5 As String, to do this in one line. Just remember this for the time being. We'll look at this again in a while.

In lines 47 to 51 we assign a value to each variable.

In lines 55 to 66 we write the values to the console as we did with *For Loops* in the previous subroutine.

We could actually have done this in a shorter way by assigning the values to the variables in each Dim statement. That would have made lines 47 to 51 redundant. Coming back to the commented line we spoke about a bit earlier, just remember that you cannot in that instance assign values in the dim statement.

In the examples we used, there's not a really big difference in the number of lines in each, however, it doesn't mean that we could do away with arrays entirely. As stated previously the real benefit would be when we have a large number of variables.

Some more examples.

In the following program example, we'll use two one-dimensional arrays to manipulate names and personnel numbers. (There are better ways to do this as we'll see later.)

Program: Arrays Example 1

```
01 Namespace Arrays
02    Class Arrays
03       Shared Sub Main()
04          SetUpConsole("Arrays 1 Example")
05          Arr()
06       End Sub
07
08       Shared Sub Arr()
09          Dim names As String() = {"Peter", "Mary", "Paul", "John",
10                                        "Margie"}
11          Dim numbers As Integer() = {123456, 654332, 987654, 654789,
```

```
12                                    852741}
13
14          Console.WriteLine("Normal Order" & vbCrLf)
15          DisplayData(names, numbers)
16
17          Console.WriteLine("Sorted Order" & vbCrLf)
18          Array.Sort(names)
19          DisplayData(names, numbers)
20      End Sub
21
22      Shared Sub DisplayData(names1 As String(), numbers1 As Integer())
23
24          Dim subs As Integer = 0
25
26          For subs = 0 To UBound(names1)
27              Console.Write(" ")
28              Console.WriteLine(numbers1(subs) &
29                              " " & names1(subs))
30          Next
31          Console.WriteLine()
32          Console.WriteLine("Press Enter to continue" & vbCrLf)
33
34          Console.ReadKey()
35      End Sub
36
37      Shared Sub SetUpConsole(name As String)
38          Console.Title = name
39          Console.BackgroundColor = ConsoleColor.White
40          Console.ForegroundColor = ConsoleColor.Black
41          Console.Clear()
42      End Sub
43   End Class
44 End Namespace
```

Output: Arrays Example 1

```
Arrays 1 Example
Normal Order

  123456  Peter
  654332  Mary
  987654  Paul
  654789  John
  852741  Margie

Press Enter to continue

Sorted Order

  123456  John
  654332  Margie
  987654  Mary
  654789  Paul
  852741  Peter

Press Enter to continue
```

Discussion: Arrays Example 1

As usual the lines have been numbered, and we'll only look at new code and concepts.

In line 5 we call a subroutine called Arr() without any parameter.

In line 8 we declare the subroutine Arr() as shared. Shared Sub Arr(). In other words, it has a class-wide scope.

Lines 9 & 10 declare an array called *names* as a string array and assign five string values, representing personnel names, to it. Dim names As String() = {"Peter", "Mary", "Paul", "John", "Margie"}. We do not specify the number of segments because it is taken from the number of values we assigned.

Lines 11 & 12 declare an array called *numbers* as an integer array and assign five integer values, representing personnel numbers, to it. Dim numbers As Integer() = {123456, 654332, 987654, 654789, 12852741}. Again, we do not specify the number of segments because it is taken from the number of values we assigned.

Line 15 calls the subroutine *DisplayData* with two parameters, which contain the two arrays described above. DisplayData(names, numbers).

In line 18 we call the sort routine of an array object with the array *names* as a parameter. Array.Sort(names). The array object inherits from the *System.Array* class and thus have a *sort method* that sorts the elements in the array in ascEnding order.

In line 19, DisplayData(names, numbers), we again call the subroutine *DisplayData* with the same parameters as previously.

The subroutine *DisplayData* is declared as shared in line 22, Shared Sub DisplayData(names1 As String(), numbers1 As Integer()), and makes provision for two arrays passed to it from the caller. The first is called names1 and is of the type string, and the second is called numbers1 and is of the type integer.

In line 24, Dim subs As Integer = 0, we declare an integer variable called *subs* to be used as the subscript (index) of the array and initialize it to zero.

The For loop in line 26, For subs = 0 To UBound(names1), starts at 0 and iterates to the upper bound subscript of the array *names1*. In other words, from 0 to 4.

NB If you look closely at the output, you will see an error. What is it?

That's correct. Only the names have been sorted and not the numbers associated with the names. To overcome this there are several options we can take, but we'll do that at a later stage.

The next example we'll look at uses the same array object as seen in line 18 of the previous example, but here we'll sort the array in ascEnding as well as descEnding format.

Program: Arrays Example 2

```
01 Namespace Arrays
02    Class Arrays
03       Shared aNames() As String = {"Peter", "Mary", "Paul", "John",
04                                              "Margie"}
05       Shared Sub Main()
06          SetUpConsole("Arrays Example 2")
07          Arr()
08       End Sub
09
10       Shared Sub Arr()
11          Dim index As Integer
12          Dim names1 = {"Peter", "Mary", "Paul", "John", "Margie"}
13
14          For index = 0 To 4
15             Console.Write((index + 1) & ". ")
16             Console.WriteLine(aNames(index))
17          Next
18
19          Console.WriteLine()
20
21          Console.WriteLine("Normal Order" & vbCrLf)
22          DisplayNames(names1)
23
24          Console.WriteLine("Sorted Order" & vbCrLf)
25          Array.Sort(names1)
26          DisplayNames(names1)
27
28          Console.WriteLine("Reversed Sorted Order" & vbCrLf)
29          Array.Reverse(names1)
30          DisplayNames(names1)
31       End Sub
32
```

```
33      Shared Sub DisplayNames(names1 As Array)
34          For Each name In names1
35              Console.Write(" ")
36              Console.WriteLine(name)
37          Next
38          Console.WriteLine()
39          Console.WriteLine("Press Enter to continue" & vbCrLf)
40          Console.ReadKey()
41      End Sub
42
43      Shared Sub SetUpConsole(name As String)
44          Console.Title = name
45          Console.BackgroundColor = ConsoleColor.White
46          Console.ForegroundColor = ConsoleColor.Black
47          Console.Clear()
48      End Sub
49  End Class
50 End Namespace
```

Output: Arrays Example 2

```
Arrays 1 Example
1. Peter
2. Mary
3. Paul
4. John
5. Margie

Normal Order

  Peter
  Mary
  Paul
  John
  Margie

Press Enter to continue
```

```
Arrays 1 Example
Sorted Order

  John
  Margie
  Mary
  Paul
  Peter

Press Enter to continue

Reversed Sorted Order

  Peter
  Paul
  Mary
  Margie
  John

Press Enter to continue
```

Discussion: Arrays 2 Example

As usual the lines have been numbered and we'll only look at new code and concepts.

In line 25, Array.Sort(names1), we call the sort routine as before with names1 as the array to be sorted in ascEnding order.

In line 29, Array.Reverse(names1), we now reverse the array to be in descEnding order.

As you can see the rest of the code is old news.

The next example has a bit more meat on the bones, so to speak. Here we will add some names to the already populated array. When we've added the names we wanted, we'll print the values of the whole array to the screen.

We will make use of some subroutines and also a function.

Program: Arrays Example 3

```
01 Namespace Arrays02
02   Class Arrays
03       Shared aNames() As String = {"Peter", "Mary", "Paul", "John",
04                                    "Margie"}
05       Shared Sub Main()
06           Dim answer As String = "n"
07           Dim names1 = aNames
08
09           SetUpConsole("Arrays Example 3")
10           Console.WriteLine("Enter y to add a name")
11
12           answer = Console.ReadKey().KeyChar
13           Console.Clear()
14
15           While answer = "y"
16               AddName(aNames)
17               Console.WriteLine("Enter y to add another name, press" &
```

```
18                                    " enter to stop")
19           answer = Console.ReadKey().KeyChar
20           Console.Clear()
21       End While
22       Console.WriteLine("Original Names" & vbCrLf)
23       DisplayNames(names1)
24       DisplayNames(aNames)
25    End Sub
26
27    Shared Sub AddName(ByRef aNames() As String)
28       Dim top As Integer = UBound(aNames) + 1
29       ReDim Preserve aNames(top)
30       aNames(top) = GetName()
31    End Sub
32
33    Shared Function GetName() As String
34       Dim name As String
35       Console.WriteLine("Enter a new name and press return: " &
36                         vbCrLf)
37       name = Console.ReadLine()
38       Console.WriteLine()
39       Return name
40    End Function
41
42    Shared Sub DisplayNames(names1 As String())
43       For Each name In names1
44          Console.Write("  ")
45          Console.WriteLine(name)
46       Next
47       Console.WriteLine()
48       Console.WriteLine("Press Enter to continue" & vbCrLf)
49       Console.ReadKey()
50    End Sub
51
```

```
52        Shared Sub SetUpConsole(name As String)
53            Console.Title = name
54            Console.BackgroundColor = ConsoleColor.White
55            Console.ForegroundColor = ConsoleColor.Black
56            Console.Clear()
57        End Sub
58     End Class
59 End Namespace
```

Output: Arrays Example 3

```
■ Add name to aNames

Oiginal Names

  Peter
  Mary
  Paul
  John
  Margie

Press Enter to continue

  Peter
  Mary
  Paul
  John
  Margie
  Nancy
  Madonna
  Henry
  William
  Kate

Press Enter to continue
```

Discussion: Arrays Example 3

In line 6, Dim answer As String = "n", we set up a so-called *flag* to use as a **sentinel value** to stop the adding of names.

Line 7, Dim names1 = aNames, creates an array called names1 and is initiated with the global array *aNames*.

In line 12, answer = Console.ReadKey().KeyChar, uses the ReadKey method that you're familiar with to read a character from the console. Because ReadKey() reads a character type (Char) it normally isn't compatible with a string type, but if we use the KeyChar property it converts the input automatically to type string.

In line 15, While answer = "y", we start a while loop that will keep executing while the variable *answer* is equal to "y".

Line 16, AddName(aNames), calls a subroutine called *AddName()* to add a name to our existing array *aNames*.

Please note that the first read statement (line 12) is outside the loop, and then again at the end of the loop in line 19. This in fact, is necessary to process all of the names we want to enter.

Line 20, Console.Clear(), clears the console for the next name.

In line 27, Shared Sub AddName(ByRef aNames() As String), we declare a shared subroutine called *AddName*, and we accept the string array *aNames* by reference (ByRef). With this reference we enable the subroutine to change the values of the array directly. In other words, *every change we make here will reflect directly in the array aNames().* If we don't do this the *aNames* in the parameter will be seen as local to the subroutine and we cannot access it outside of this subroutine.

In line 28, Dim top As Integer = UBound(aNames) + 1, we declare an integer variable called 'top', and assign the upper bound value of the array plus one to it. We do this because we want to enlarge the existing array 'aNames' by one segment.

The statement, ReDim Preserve aNames(top), in line 29 re-dimensions (ReDim) the array to contain segments from 0 to one more than it was. The Preserve statement preserves the existing values stored in the array. If we don't use Preserve all the values in the existing array would be destroyed.

In line 30, aNames(top) = GetName(), we call the function *GetName()* and assign the value returned by that function to the last segment (aNames(top)) of the array *aNames()*.

In line 33, Shared Function GetName() As String, we declare a function called *GetName* of the type string. In other words, it will return a string value to the caller.

In line 37, name = Console.ReadLine(), we read a value from the console and store it into the variable *name*.

The statement, Return name, in line 39 returns the value stored in *name* to the caller. Remember, this will be a string because of the type the function was declared to be.

The rest of the code we've seen quite a lot already and is thus self-explanatory.

In the **next example** we will solve the problem of sorting one array and keep the data from another together with the values in the first array.

There are different ways to do this, but we're going to use a bubble sort algorithm.

Let's look at how we will do it without programming. Say we have 4 values, 6,3,5,1. Okay we know how to do this. Scan the numbers for the smallest one and note it. In this case 1. Now get the first value bigger than 1 which is 3, the next is 5 and the largest 6. So, 1,3,5,6.

This is easy for us humans. We instinctively know how to do it, but the computer doesn't. With the bubble sort we compare the first two numbers. If the second of the two is smaller than the first, we swap them around. Now we have 3,6,5,1. We then compare the second and third numbers. In our case 5 is less than 6 so we swap them. Now we have 3,5,6,1. Compare the third and fourth numbers. One is smaller than six, so we do the swap. We now have 3,5,1,6. Obviously the list is not yet sorted so we start the process again, but as the highest number is now at the bottom of the list, we don't have to look at it again. Why the bubble sort name then? In this way the smallest value bubbles up to the top and the largest sinks to the bottom, each time we pass through the loop.

Let's look at our example where we want to take the number with the name as we sort the names.

Program: Sort Example

```
01 Namespace Arrays
02    Class Arrays
03       Shared number() As Integer = {123456, 654332, 987654, 654789,
04                                         852741}
05       Shared name() As String = {"Peter", "Mary", "Paul", "John","Margie"}
06
07       Shared Sub Main()
08          SetUpConsole("Sort on Name and Number Comes With")
09          DisplayNames(number, name)
10          BubbleSort(number, name)
11          DisplayNames(number, name)
12       End Sub
13
14       Shared Sub BubbleSort(number() As Integer, name() As String)
15          Dim top As Integer = UBound(name)
16          Dim inner As Integer       'Inner loop subscript
17          Dim outer As Integer       'Outer loop subscript
18          Dim nameTemp As String
19          Dim numTemp As Integer
20
21          For outer = 0 To top
22             For inner = 0 To (top - 1)
23                If name(inner) > name(inner + 1) Then
24                   nameTemp = name(inner)
```

```vbnet
25              numTemp = number(inner)
26              name(inner) = name(inner + 1)
27              number(inner) = number(inner + 1)
28              name(inner + 1) = nameTemp
29              number(inner + 1) = numTemp
30          End If
31        Next inner
32      Next outer
33    End Sub
34
35    Shared Sub DisplayNames(number1() As Integer,
36                              name1() As String)
37      Dim subs As Integer
38      For subs = 0 To UBound(name1)
39          Console.Write(" " & number1(subs) & " ")
40          Console.WriteLine(name1(subs))
41      Next
42      Console.WriteLine()
43      Console.WriteLine("Press Enter to continue" & vbCrLf)
44      Console.ReadKey()
45    End Sub
46
47    Shared Sub SetUpConsole(name As String)
48      Console.Title = name
49      Console.BackgroundColor = ConsoleColor.White
50      Console.ForegroundColor = ConsoleColor.Black
51      Console.Clear()
52    End Sub
53
54  End Class
55 End Namespace
```

Output: Sort Example

```
  ▆ Sort on Name and Number Comes With

   123456   Peter
   654332   Mary
   987654   Paul
   654789   John
   852741   Margy

Press Enter to continue

   654789   John
   852741   Margy
   654332   Mary
   987654   Paul
   123456   Peter

Press Enter to continue
```

Discussion: Sort Example

This program is very much the same as the previous one. We've just added a bubble sort routine called BubbleSort(). We'll make use of nested loops. In other words, a loop within another loop.

Let's look at the new code:

In line 10, BubbleSort(number, name), we call the bubble sort routine and pass the two arrays *number* and *name* to it.

Line 14, Shared Sub BubbleSort(number() As Integer, name() As String), declares the bubble sort routine and accepts the arrays *number()* and *name()* as parameters.

Line 15, Dim top As Integer = UBound(name), declares an integer variable called *top*. This contains the index of the last segment of the array. In our case it is 4.

Lines 16 and 17 declare integer variables to use as subscripts for our two arrays.

In lines 18 and 19 we declare variables to contain the values of the correct segment temporarily when we swap them around.

Note that in the for statement in line 22, For inner = 0 To (top - 1), we subtract one from the largest subscript to make sure that the subscript doesn't go out of bounds (larger than the subscript for the last segment in the array).

The if statement starting in line 23, If name(inner) > name(inner + 1) Then, compares the values of the names in adjacent segments of the array *names()*. Remember we're sorting on the names.

Lines 24 to 26 swaps the names around.

Lines 27 to 29 swap the numbers in the corresponding segments around to keep the correct name and number together in their arrays.

To make more sense of this code do a dry run on paper to see what is happening.

To do a dry run you write down the names of the variables with their values on paper. Now imagine you're the computer. Read the first line of code (in the bubble sort routine) and write down the values. Now do the same for the next line. Remember to increment the values as you go through the loop. Keep on doing that until the last line. This will give you a good idea of what is happening step by step.

Fun Facts

Few companies that installed computers to reduce the employment of clerks have realized their expectations.... They now need more, and more expensive clerks even though they call them "operators" or "programmers." ~Peter F. Drucker

All programmers are playwrights and all computers are lousy actors. ~Author Unknown

Always code as if the guy who ends up maintaining your code will be a violent psychopath who knows where you live. ~Martin Golding

Everyone knows that debugging is twice as hard as writing a program in the first place. So if you are as clever as you can be when you write it, how will you ever debug it? ~Brian Kernighan

Sometimes it pays to stay in bed on Monday, rather than spending the rest of the week debugging Monday's code. ~Dan Salomon

And then it occurred to me that a computer is a stupid machine with the ability to do incredibly smart things, while computer programmers are smart people with the ability to do incredibly stupid things. They are, in short, a perfect match. ~Bill Bryson

Another effective technique is to explain your code to someone else. This will often cause you to explain the bug to yourself. Sometimes it takes no more than a few sentences, followed by an embarrassed "Never mind, I see what's wrong. Sorry to bother you." This works remarkably well; you can even use non-programmers as listeners. One university computer center kept a teddy bear near the help desk. Students with mysterious bugs were required to explain them to the bear before they could speak to a human counselor. ~Brian Kernighan and Rob Pike, about debugging

CHAPTER 9

PROGRAMMING

I know you're burning to start, but before that we must briefly discuss some conventions.

First of all, you must take note of the fact that VB *code* is case insensitive. That means that an uppercase letter is not distinct from a lowercase letter. That means "Name" and "name" is seen as the same thing.

Anywhere on a line you can place a comment by preceding it with a single quote ('). Anything after the single quote will be seen as comments and will be ignored by the compiler.

The first programming principle

Stay Calm

Any grouping of code must end with the End statement as in

> Shared sub Main
> ' …..
> End Sub

The declaration and End statement should be alone on a line to enhance reading.

Use identifiers that make sense; firstName not fiNa etc.

Use **Pascal Casing** for class names and method names.

Use **camel Casing** for method arguments and local variables.

Pascal case is a subset of Camel **Case** where the first letter is capitalized. For example, userAccount is a camel **case** and UserAccount is a **Pascal case**.

Declare all member variables at the top of the class. Start variables with the first three letters of the type it represents. It will help with maintenance later.

So, at last, we can start to try out some programming using Visual Studio Community 2019.

In this example we're only going to use easy statements and only Console Applications. These applications take input directly from the keyboard and display output directly on the screen. The examples you have seen in the previous chapters were all of this type.

Getting Started With Visual Studio Community 2019

First of all, you must open the version of Visual Studio Community 2019 that you downloaded and installed.

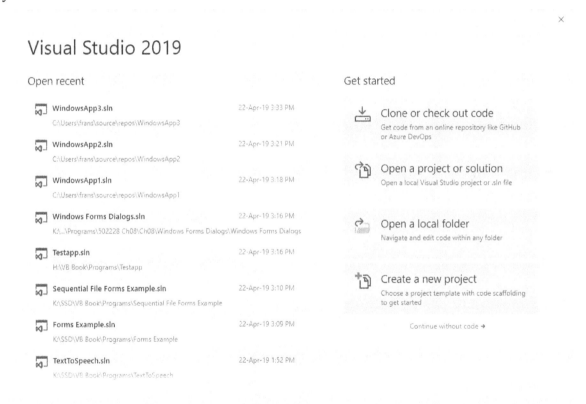

This is how it displays on my computer. Yours may look different. Choose the Create a New Project option.

This is what will be displayed next:

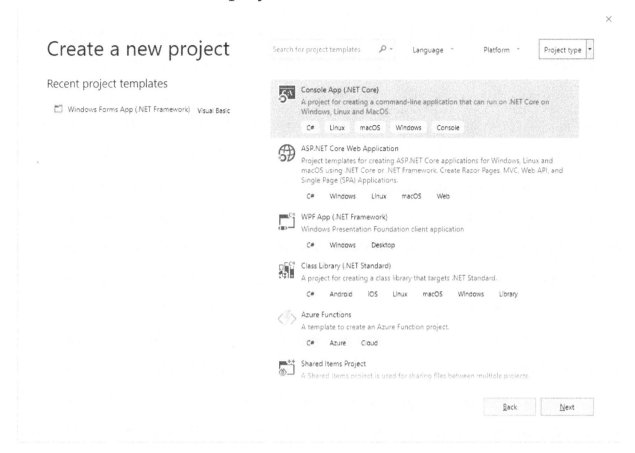

At the top right click at the down arrow on *Project type* and choose *console*.

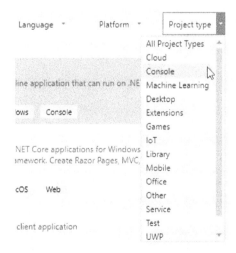

Now click on the down arrow for *Language* and select *Visual Basic*.

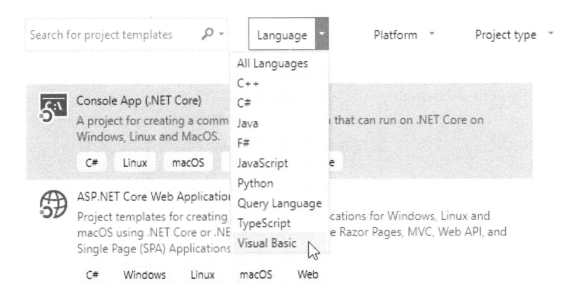

The next screen wil look like this:

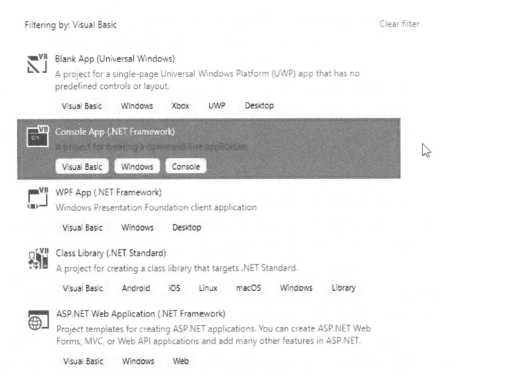

Choose *Console App (.NTE Framework)*.

The following screen will appear.

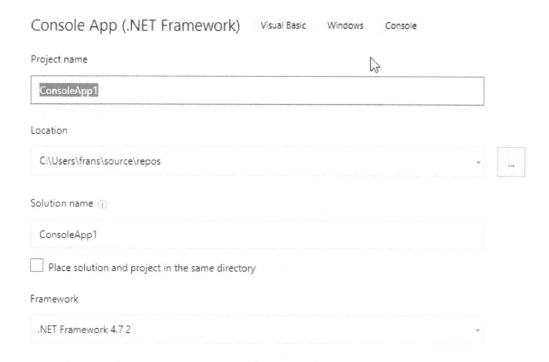

Here we must configure the project.

Enter the project *Name*, the *location* where it must be stored, and the name of the *Solution*. As you can see in the screen above the information is completed already, but doesn't say very much. Change the information to your own.

Next click on the *create* button.

The following is what you get:

```
Module Module1

      Sub Main()

      End Sub

End Module
```

Already supplied statements

You have a new program, but in that format, it will not do anything. You have a **Module** called Module1 and a **method** called *Main*. Every Console program in VB must have at least one method declared as *Main()*.

Note

Scope in VB refers to a region of code in which a method or variable is visible to the rest of the code in the same scope.

In the examples so far, we started with a class each time, so what is this new thing called Module?

Modules are just named containers for code, and all code must be in some kind of module. At their simplest, they are a way to organize your routines into meaningful groups.

The most basic, the so-called "Modules" (or "code modules" as they were once called to distinguish them from the more general concept of modules) provide little more than that, plus a way to declare variables that live outside of any single routine and don't go away when you exit the routine, and an easy way to associate which code/module(s) are in which source files.

Classes are a more powerful type of Module that can be "Instanced", which just means that you can treat them like a data type, create multiple copies of them with different values/contents, assign them to variables, pass them to and from functions and other methods, etc. These copies or "instances" are more commonly called "Objects".

Modules are used in VB mostly as a code repository where generic code is stored that is accessible application-wide. Modules are **not** objects; they're nothing more than a place to store code. A class module on the other hand **is** an object and this is probably their biggest difference from standard modules.

Both modules and classes are used to group statements that belong together. The main difference between the two is that a class can be instantiated and a module not. In other words, a class can be used to store data for each object created from that class. E.g., Child1 have its own name, surname, birth date etc. and so does child2 and child3. Each of these can be referred to separately and changes in one will not affect any of the others. To elaborate a bit further, we can create a class Person and then declare child1/2/3 as Person. Then declare Persons as a list of person. Each of the children can then be added to the list and so can any Object with the same attributes as Person.

With a module we can also create variables for name, surname etc. but any changes to one variable will be reflected throughout the scope of that module. One may argue that we have to create different variables for each child in the class in any case, and thus we can just as well create variables for each child in the module. On the face of things, it will seem as if the amount of work is the same, but it's not. For maybe one or two variables, it's the same, but suppose we have 10 different variables for each child, and we have 100 children, then we will have to declare 1000 variables. In a class we declare 10 variables and then we can have 100 instantiations. In that case we'll end up with 110 statements instead of 1000.

There are also other differences, as we know that we can inherit attributes from a base class, but we cannot inherit from a module.

VB supplies the module automatically when we open a project, but because of the limited capabilities of the module, I usually use only classes.

There are obviously a lot more to both the module and the class than explained here, but for the scope of this book it is enough.

The body of a class or a method must occur between the declaration and the end statement. For example:

```
Public Class Employee

    Statement list

        "

        "

    End Class
```

The statements Sub Main() and End Sub creates a method called Main. The brackets () can be used when the method Main must receive parameters.

The parenthesis () are usually used to specify/send parameters. The line, Console.WriteLine("Method without parameters") specifies the text "Method without parameters" as a parameter for the WriteLine method.

If a method does not make use of parameters, we must still show that with empty parenthesis ().

OK, it's fine to display something on the screen, but not very useful. So, we must be able to enter something, store it in a variable, manipulate it in some way and then display the answer in a meaningful way.

The following program uses the method InputMethod, to read input from the console, and the method OutputMethod, with a parameter, to display whatever is passed to it from the console.

Program: Read Write Example

```vb
01  Namespace ReadWrite
02    Class ProgramInput
03      Shared yourName As String
04
05      Shared Sub Main()
06
07        SetUpConsole("Program ReadWrite")
08
09        OutputMethod("Not Entered")
10        yourName = InputMethod()
11        OutputMethod(yourName)
12
13        Console.WriteLine("Press Any Key")
14        Console.ReadKey()
15      End Sub
16
17      Shared Sub SetUpConsole(name)
18        Console.Title = name
19        Console.BackgroundColor = ConsoleColor.White
20        Console.ForegroundColor = ConsoleColor.Black
21        Console.Clear()
22      End Sub
23
```

```
24    Shared Sub OutputMethod(name As String)
25        Console.Write("Your Name Is ")
26        Console.WriteLine(name)
27        Console.WriteLine()
28    End Sub
29
30    Shared Function InputMethod() As String
31        Dim temp As String
32        Console.WriteLine()
33        Console.WriteLine("Please Enter Your" &
34                          "Name and Press Return")
35        temp = Console.ReadLine()
36        Console.WriteLine()
37        Return temp
38    End Function
39  End Class
40 End Namespace
```

Output: Read Write Example

```
Program ReadWrite

Your Name Is Not Entered


Please Enter Your Name and Press Return
Long John Silver

Your Name Is Long John Silver

Press Any Key
```

Discussion: Read Write Example

In line 3, Shared yourName As String, we declare a variable *yourName* of the type *String*. You will see that we didn't use the Dim statement to declare the variable, because we want it to be global so that we can use it anywhere in the program.

Line 9, OutputMethod("Not Entered"), calls OutputMethod with a literal value as a parameter.

Line 10, yourName = InputMethod(), assigns the value returned by the function *InputMethod* to the variable *yourName*. (Note the use of Camel Casing in the name of the variable.)

Line 24, Shared Sub OutputMethod(name As String), has the declaration of the method *OutputMethod*. It accepts the value of the parameter from the calling statement in the variable *name*. The variable *name* is declared as string in the receiving parameter. This is not strictly necessary but will make the code easier to read and limit the chances of an error.

In line 30, Shared Function InputMethod() As String, we declare a global function called *InputMethod* and assign the type *String* to it. This means that it will return a string value to be assigned to the variable in the caller.

In lines 33, Console.WriteLine("Please Enter Your" &, and 34, "Name and Press Return"), calls *Console.WriteLine* with a literal parameter. What is interesting here is the fact that we broke the literal value of the parameter up into two lines. This was done by closing the string and using the & to concatenate what follows on the next line. Remember to start the string with a quotation mark.

Line 35, temp = Console.ReadLine(), reads a value from the console and assigns it to the variable *temp*.

In line 37, Return temp, we use the *Return* statement to return the value we want to the caller.

What about reading two numbers from the console, use a method to multiply them, and display the answer?

Program: Read Multiply and Display Example

```
01  Namespace ReadMultiplyAndDisplay
02    Class Program
03      Shared Sub Main()
04
05        Dim conString As String = "Enter " &
06                      "an integer per line " & vbLf
07        Dim firstVal As Integer
08        Dim secondVal As Integer
09
10        SetUpConsole("Read Multiply " & "And Display")
11        Console.WriteLine(conString)
12
13        conString = Console.ReadLine()
14        firstVal = Convert.ToInt16(conString)
15        conString = Console.ReadLine()
16        secondVal = Convert.ToInt16(conString)
17
18        Console.Write("The answer is = ")
19
20        conString = Calc(firstVal, secondVal)
21
22
23        Console.WriteLine(conString)
24        conString = Console.ReadLine()
25      End Sub
26
```

```
27        Shared Function Calc(x As Integer, y As Integer) As String
28
29          Dim answer As Integer
30
31          answer = x * y
32
33          Return answer
34
35      End Function
36
37      Shared Sub SetUpConsole(name)
38          Console.Title = name
39          Console.BackgroundColor = ConsoleColor.White
40          Console.ForegroundColor = ConsoleColor.Black
41          Console.Clear()
42      End Sub
43   End Class
44 End Namespace
```

Output: Read Multiply and Display Example

```
Read Multiply And Display

Enter an integer per line

663
100
The answer is = 66300
```

Of course, there are other and maybe better ways to do this, but let's keep it simple.

Discussion: Read Multiply and Display Example

In line 06, "an integer per line " & vbLf, the VB constant *vbLf* has been concatenated to the literal value. This is one of the output manipulation statements and forces the control to a new line. When this is used with the writeline statement, the writeline statement places control at the start of the following line, and the linefeed constant (vbLf) advances to the next line, which results in a blank line in the output.

We use the Convert statement in lines 14, Convert.ToInt16(conString), and 16, Convert.ToInt16(conString), to change the string value read from the console (conString) to an integer value so it can be assigned to the integer variables.

In line 18, Console.Write("The answer is = "), we use the *Write* method of the console class. We have seen that the Writeline statement forces the cursor to a new line. With the Write statement the cursor stays on the same line, so whatever goes to the console next will be displayed on the same line.

In line 20, conString = Calc(firstVal, secondVal), we assign the value returned by the *Calc* function to the string value conString. It is important to note that in previous programs we had to convert the integer value that was returned to a string value before we could assign it to a string variable. Why not here?

The answer lies in the way we declared our *Calc* function.

In lines 27 to 35 we created a function to multiply two values and return the answer to the calling method.

Let's look at line 27, Shared Function Calc(x As Integer, y As Integer) As String, first. The function is declared as *Shared*, so it can be seen in the whole class. Next, we specified two parameters of the type integer, and then we **declare the function as type String**. It is because of this that we didn't have to convert the returned value to a string type to assign it to a string variable. More about this a little bit later.

Line 29, Dim answer As Integer, declares the variable *answer* as type integer. We use *Dim* and not *Shared*, because we want the variable to be local to the function.

Line 31, answer = x * y, multiply the variables x and y (specified as Integer) and assigns the resulting value to the variable *answer*.

The punchline is line 33, Return answer, where we return our integer value stored in *answer* to the calling module. Because we declared our function as type *String*, the conversion of *answer* to type string is done implicitly and we don't have to do it ourselves.

Line 35, End Function, ends the function.

The following VB constants can be used to include something other than the literal value between the quotation marks that demarcate the start and the end of the string. We use the concatenation symbol & to add the constant to the string.

- vbCrLf = "\n"   # Carriage return linefeed combination
- vbCr = chr(13)   # Carriage return character
- vbLf = chr(10)   # Linefeed character
- vbNewLine = "\n"   # Platform-specific new line character; whichever is appropriate for current platform
- vbNullChar = chr(0)   # Character having value 0
- vbNullString = chr(0)   # String having value 0. Not the same as a zero-length string (""); used for calling external procedures
- vbObjectError = -2147221504   # User-defined error umbers should be greater than this value. For example: Err.Raise Number = vbObjectError + 1000
- vbTab = chr(9)   # Tab character
- vbBack = chr(8)   # Backspace character
- vbFormFeed = chr(12)   # Not useful in Microsoft Windows
- vbVerticalTab = chr(11) # Not useful in Microsoft Windows

You can play around with these constants to see the effect of each.

A comprehensive list of VB Constants can be found at this link:

http://vb2py.sourceforge.net/docs/vbconstants.html

The previous program is good and well, as it only has to produce an answer to a question. If we want to display for instance, employee data, it will be quite a drag to re-enter the data every time we want to display it, and this is where the concept of files comes in.

The following program is the same as the one we've seen under the file section, so let's look at it in more detail:

Program: File Handling Example

```vbnet
01  imports System.IO 'Needed for StreamReader and Streamwriter
02
03  Namespace FileHandlingExample
04    Class Program
05      Shared Sub Main()
06        Dim lines As String = "Hi there, my dear old friend" & vbCrLf
07        Dim file As StreamWriter
08
09        file = My.Computer.FileSystem.OpenTextFileWriter("D:/test.txt",
10                                                            False)
11        file.WriteLine(lines)
12        file.Close()
13
14        Dim fileReader As StreamReader
15
16        fileReader=My.Computer.FileSystem.OpenTextFileReader(
17                                                  "D:/test.txt")
18
19        Dim text As String = fileReader.ReadToEnd()
20
```

```vbnet
21          fileReader.Close()
22
23          Console.WriteLine(text)
24
25          Using file1 As New StreamWriter("D:/test.txt", True)
26              file1.WriteLine("How are you?")
27          End Using
28
29          Dim text1 As String
30
31          Using fileReader1 As New StreamReader("D:/test.txt")
32              text1 = fileReader1.ReadToEnd()
33          End Using
34
35          Console.WriteLine(text1)
36          Console.ReadKey()
37      End Sub
38
39      Shared Sub SetUpConsole(name As String)
40          Console.Title = name
41          Console.BackgroundColor = ConsoleColor.White
42          Console.ForegroundColor = ConsoleColor.Black
43          Console.Clear()
44      End Sub
45  End Class
46 End Namespace
```

Output: File Handling Example

File Handling Example

```
Hi there, my dear old friend


Hi there, my dear old friend

How are you?
```

Discussion: File Handling Example

01 Imports System.IO

This statement imports the System.IO namespace needed for the file handling that we're going to do.

06   Dim lines As String = "Hi there, " & "my dear old friend" & vbCrLf assigns a literal value to the string variable called lines. Let's recap. The & concatenates what follows to the string and constant vbCrLf moves the cursor to the start of a new line. Cr means write a carriage return (the same as pressing the enter key on the keyboard), and we already know Lf means go to a new line.

07   Dim file As StreamWriter

This statement uses the *StreamWriter* class from the namespace System.IO. It creates the object instance *file,* of the type *StreamWriter*.

09   file = My.Computer.FileSystem.OpenTextFileWriter("D:/test.txt",

10   False)

This uses the *StreamWriter* class from the namespace *System.IO*. It creates the object instance file of the type *StreamWriter*, and connects it to the physical file *test.txt* on the D: drive. If we don't specify the drive as in (test.txt) it will use the path of the current directory.

11   file.WriteLine(lines)

This statement uses *WriteLine*, but not to write to the console, but to write the contents of the string called *lines* to the file called *file* as stated above. It ends by writing a newline and a carriage return as specified in the string *lines* that we built in line 6.

12   file.Close()

This statement closes the file on the disk. Something to note here is that if we do not close the file the contents would not be written to the disk. This happens because the content is written to a buffer in memory and only "flushed" to the disk when the code reaches the close statement. It would also create an error later in the program when we use a new *StreamWriter.*

14   Dim fileReader As StreamReader

This statement opens the same file as before, but this time for reading and not for writing. It uses the *StreamReader* class and creates a StreamReader called *streamReader*. *Notice the one is spelled with a capital letter "S" and the other with a lowercase letter "s".*

16   fileReader=My.Computer.FileSystem.OpenTextFileReader(

17   "D:/test.txt")

This statement split over two lines, connects the *fileReader* to file *D:/test.txt* to prepare it for reading.

19   Dim text As String = fileReader.ReadToEnd()

This statement reads the file to its end, and assigns the contents to the string variable called *text.*

21   fileReader.Close()

This closes the StreamReader called *fileReader.*

26   Console.WriteLine(text)

We know this statement from before. It writes the contents of the string *text* to the console. As the StreamReader read everything in the file, it includes the VB Constants. The output will look precisely as it did when we wrote it to the file.

25   Using **file1** As New StreamWriter("D:/test.txt", True)

This uses a *Using* block to group the needed resources and ends with the End Using statement in line 27. As seen above it creates a new instantiation of the *StreamWriter* (As New), and connects it to our file on the disk. Here we have a new concept represented by the True parameter. This opens the file, but places control after the last character in the file. Everything written to the file gets added at the back. When we opened the StreamWriter before, we used the *False* parameter which resulted in the contents of the file being discarded. When we leave this parameter out it defaults to *False*.

26   file1.WriteLine("How are you?")

This adds the string value to the end of *file1*.

Something to note here is that we had to close the file in line 12, or else the contents would not be physically written to the file. Because we're using the *Using* statement in this case, we do not actually have to close the file. All the resources between the *Using* and *End Using* statements would be closed and disposed from memory automatically.

31   Using **fileReader1** As New **System.IO.**StreamReader("D:/test.txt")

These statements connect a new instance of *fileReader1* as a *StreamReader* and connects it to the file on disk.

32   text1 = fileReader1.ReadToEnd()

Here we read the file from start to end and assign the contents to the String variable *text1*.

33   End Using

This ends the block of code.

OK, just to conclude, let's look at another program that will tie the loose ends in file handling together. Here we will enter information for employees on the console and write it to a file. We will then read the contents of the file and display it on the console.

Program: Read and Write Sequential File Example

```
01  Imports System.IO
02  Namespace ReadWriteSequentialFile
03    Public Class Employee
04      Public empNum As Integer
05      Public name As String
06      Public salary As Double
07    End Class
08
09    Public Class ReadWriteSequentialFile
10
11      Shared Sub Main()
12        Const cEnd As Integer = 999
13        Const delim As String = ","
14        Const fileName As String = "D:\EmployeeData.txt"
15
16        Dim outfile As StreamWriter
17        Dim emp As New Employee
18
19        SetUpConsole("Read and Write a Sequential File")
20
21        Using FS As New FileStream(fileName, FileMode.Append,
22                                          FileAccess.Write)
23          outfile = New StreamWriter(FS)
24
25          Console.Write("Enter employee number or " & cEnd &
26                          " to quit » ")
27          emp.empNum = Convert.ToInt32(Console.ReadLine())
28
```

```
29          While (emp.empNum <> cEnd)
30              Console.Write("Enter last name » ")
31              emp.name = Console.ReadLine()
32              Console.Write("Enter salary » ")
33              emp.salary = Convert.ToDouble(Console.ReadLine())
34              outfile.WriteLine(emp.empNum & delim &
35                                emp.name & delim & emp.salary)
36              Console.Write("Enter next employee number or " &
37                                cEnd & " to quit » ")
38              emp.empNum = Convert.ToInt32(Console.ReadLine())
39          End While
40          outfile.Close()
41      End Using
42      Dim reader As StreamReader
43      Dim recordIn As String
44      Dim fields() As String
45
46      Console.WriteLine(vbCrLf & "{0, -5} {1, -12} {2, 8}",
47                "Num", "Name", "Salary" & vbCrLf)
48
49      Using FS As New FileStream(fileName, FileMode.Open,
50                    FileAccess.Read)
51          reader = New StreamReader(FS)
52          recordIn = reader.ReadLine()
53
54          While recordIn <> ""
55              fields = recordIn.Split(delim)
56              emp.empNum = Convert.ToInt32(fields(0))
57              emp.name = fields(1)
58              emp.salary = Convert.ToDouble(fields(2))
59              Console.WriteLine("{0,-5} {1,-12} {2,10}", emp.empNum,
60                                emp.name, emp.salary.ToString("C"))
61              recordIn = reader.ReadLine()
62          End While
```

```
63          End Using
64
65              Console.ReadKey()
66      End Sub
67
68      Shared Sub SetUpConsole(name As String)
69              Console.Title = name
70              Console.BackgroundColor = ConsoleColor.White
71              Console.ForegroundColor = ConsoleColor.Black
72              Console.Clear()
73          End Sub
74      End Class
75  End Namespace
```

Output 1: Read and Write Sequential File Example

```
█▌ Read and Write a Sequential File

Enter employee number or 999 to quit » 123
Enter last name » Van Wyk
Enter salary » 10000.00
Enter next employee number or 999 to quit » 321
Enter last name » Jackson
Enter salary » 22000.00
Enter next employee number or 999 to quit » 258
Enter last name » Boycott
Enter salary » 55000.36
Enter next employee number or 999 to quit » 999
```

Output 2: Read and Write Sequential File Example

```
Num     Name            Salary

123     Van Wyk         $10,000.00
321     Jackson         $22,000.00
258     Boycott         $55,000.36
```

Discussion: Read and Write Sequential File Example

In line 1, Imports System.IO, we import the *System.IO* namespace. This statement makes the Base Class we need for *StreamReader* and *StreamWriter* available.

In line 03, Public Class Employee, we declare a class by the name of *Employee*. Remember the class is the blueprint and we will use it to create instances of the object we derive from the blueprint.

In lines 04, Public empNum As Integer, 05, Public name As String, and 06, Public salary As Double, we declare the three variables our class needs.

The first variable can receive integer values and is called *empNum*, the second can receive string values and is called *name*, and the last one can receive floating point numbers (like 3.33) and is called *salary*. We could include get and/or set statements to specify two accessors that we can use to get the instance values from the object, or send values to be stored in the instance of the object, but that's outside our scope.

Remember the *structure* that we used previously to create an object that consisted of three different types. We could assign values to the variables, and use it as a whole (the whole group), but if we wanted to do something with the values it would have had to be done outside of the structure. With our class here we could do things like validation etc. within the class itself and only pass the corrected values back. In other words, we can create other variables within the class, and include methods to work with that variables before sending the contents back to the caller. The code inside the class will then be hidden, or protected if you like, from the user.

In line 07, End Class, we end the Employee class.

The statements in lines 12, Const cEnd As Integer = 999, 13, Const delim As String = "," and 14, Const fileName As String = "D:\EmployeeData.txt", declare constants of different types. A constant is something like a variable, but we can only assign it a value in the declaration statement, and it cannot be changed afterwards.

The first constant is cEnd and contains the integer 999. Just to clarify, we cannot use *end* as a constant, because it's a Keyword and cannot be used as a variable/constant. We'll use this value (999) to compare against the employee number to see if we must continue.

The second constant is a delimiter that consists of a comma. We will use it to separate the values we write to our file.

The third one contains the name of the file we're going to work with.

Line 16, Dim outfile As StreamWriter, creates a variable *outfile* of the type *streamwriter*.

Line 17, Dim emp As New Employee, creates an instance of the class *Employee*. This instance is called *emp*. Remember the *New* statement creates a new instance.

In lines 21, Using FS As New FileStream(fileName, FileMode.Append, and 22, FileAccess.Write) we create a *using* block of code as before to create a new FileStream.

Remember StreamWriter and StreamReader? This is totally another kettle of fish. Why?

Well, with the FileStream class we can create a channel (think of a water pipe) between our program and a file on disk. Here we can specify if we want to read from the file, write to the file or append to the file, to name but a few. We can then use the StreamReader or StreamWriter with this channel to do the physical reading, writing, and manipulation of the file declared with the stream specifications.

In the statement we created a FileStream named FS as a new instance of the class FileStream, and we specify the file name, the file mode, and the file access method. As you can see the mode is append and the access is write. So, we can create the file, and we can also read from it by changing the access method.

In line 23, outfile = New StreamWriter(FS), we create a new StreamWriter called *outfile*, that uses the stream *FS* with the characteristics specified for that stream.

The Write to the screen in line 25, Console.Write("Enter employee " &, and line 26, "number or" & cEnd & " to quit » "), must be very familiar by now.

You should be familiar with the statement in line 27, emp.empNum = Convert.ToInt32(Console.ReadLine()), where we read a value from the console, convert it to an integer and store it into the *empNum* field of class instance *emp*.

Discussion: Code Segment:

```
29          While (emp.empNum <> cEnd)
30              Console.Write("Enter last name » ")
31              emp.name = Console.ReadLine()
32              Console.Write("Enter salary » ")
33              emp.salary = Convert.ToDouble(Console.ReadLine())
34              Outfile.WriteLine(emp.empNum & delim &
35                              emp.name & delim & emp.salary)
36              Console.Write("Enter next employee number or " &
37                              cEnd & " to quit » ")
38              emp.empNum = Convert.ToInt32(Console.ReadLine())
39          End While
```

We read values for *name* and *salary* for object *emp* from the console. (Remember we read the value of *empNum* in line 27.) We see an important principle here. It is called the preliminary read. If you look at the previous segment of code, you will see that we read the first employee number from the console **before** the while loop. We must do this because we check if *empNum* is not equal to *cEnd*. We declared *cEnd* to have the value of 999 remember. We must do this before we check the loop condition for the first time in order to not continue with the loop if we entered 999 to end it.

At this stage we have data for *empNum*, *name* and *salary*, so we can write it to the file. This is done using the *Writeline* method of the stream called *outfile* that we declared previously. OK, the first iteration of the loop is complete. To know if we must continue, we have to read the next *empNum* at the end of the loop, so that the loop condition can be checked to see if it must do another iteration. If we do not enter 999 from the console, the loop will continue and write the next employee's info to the file.

After the loop stops, we close the open connections in the next statement. Line 41, End Using.

That's fine. We have created a new file on the disk, and it contains the information of the employees we entered. In the file on disk it looks like this:

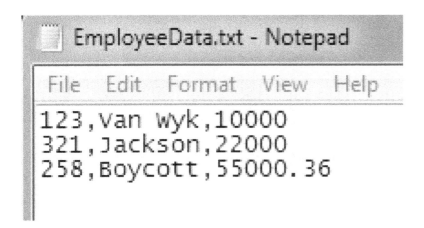

Now we're going to read the data from the file on disk, but we'll have to display it on the console in a more understandable way. Let's look at the rest of the code.

In line 42, Dim reader As StreamReader, we create a streamreader called *reader*.

In line 43, Dim recordIn As String, we create a variable called *recordIn*, in which to store the record we read from the file. It obviously is of the type *String*.

The statement in line 44, Dim fields() As String, declares the variable *fields* to be a string array. As we said before a one-dimensional array like the one we use here, will consist of a table with a number of rows. Each row will contain one line from our file. Because a row from the file consist of the combination of three values separated by commas it can be stored in a string.

In lines 46, Console.WriteLine(vbCrLf & "{0, -5} {1, -12} {2, 8}", and 47, "Num", "Name", "Salary" & vbCrLf), we set up the headings for the records that we're going to print to the screen. *vbCrLf* is old news by now, but let's look at what follows, "{0, -5} {1, -12} {2, 8}". You can define the width of the string that is inserted into the result string by using this syntax. In the first placeholder {0, -5} the zero stands for the number of the place it holds and the -5 depicts the length of the string to be inserted. The minus in front of the 5 means the string will be left justified, in other words the string will start at the leftmost character of the declared space. It is very important to note that if the string is longer than the length of the placeholder the preferred length will be ignored, and the entire string will be inserted in the result string. If the number specifying the length of the string to be inserted, ({2, 8} for example), does not have a minus in front of it the string will be right aligned in the placeholder. This means it will start from the rightmost character and fill up to the left.

Just remember that strings that are too long for the placeholder will skew the columns. There are ways to fix that, but it falls outside of our scope.

The three literals in line 47, "Num", "Name", "Salary", will be placed in the first, second and third place holder.

Line 49, Using FS As New FileStream(fileName, FileMode.Open, and line 50, FileAccess.Read), we use FileStream as before, but this time the File Mode is Open, and the File Access is read. Obviously, we're going to open the file and then read from it. In line 49 the same principle of the preliminary read followed by a loop to read the number of rows in the file is adhered to.

In line 51, reader = New StreamReader(FS), we create a new *streamreader* called *reader* and connect it to the *filestream* from lines 49 and 50.

In line 54, While recordIn <> "", we declare the start of a *While loop* where we check if the variable *recordIn*, that we assigned the contents with the *readline* functions in either line 52 or 61 to, contains any value. The <> means less than or greater than, compares the contents of *recordIn* to an empty string depicted by two sets of quotation marks next to each other. Seen as "". Remember that there is no space between the quotation marks. The outcome of this will be *True* if the variable contains anything.

After the read, a row from the file consist of the combination of three values separated by commas, and we want to space them on the console. We obviously must find a way to split them into the three different values according to the commas. Luckily a string variable has a *Split* command which we can use.

The statement in line 55, fields = recordIn.Split(delim), does exactly what we want. Remember we declared a constant *delim* as type string and placed a comma in it. Because *fields* have been declared as an array the *Split* command will place each separated item into one segment of the array.

In our example the reference to fields(0) will return the value 123, the reference to fields(1) will return Van Wyk, and the reference to fields(2) will return 10000. Fields remember, is a string array, so we must again convert the strings to the correct type to store into the properties in the Employee class. That is done in the following three statements:

```
56        emp.empNum = Convert.ToInt32(fields(0))
57        emp.name = fields(1)
58        emp.salary = Convert.ToDouble(fields(2))
```

In line 59, Console.WriteLine("{0,-5} {1,-12} {2,10}", emp.empNum, and line 60, emp.name, emp.salary.ToString("C")) we write the values we assigned in lines 56 to 58 to the console. This statement writes the values in the three segments of the array to the console. Here we specify three parameters within the curly brackets as follows: {0,-5} means the first variable will be 5 characters long and will be left justified in the string. In our case it will be written as "123 ". {1,-12} will write "Van Wyk " left justified and {2,10} will be written as 10 characters, but will be right justified as follows:

" $10,000.00". The string will be written from the right-hand edge of the column and if there are less characters than the allotted number specified it will be filled with spaces. The first value in emp.EmpNum will be written to the specification of the parameter 0, emp.Name to parameter 1 and so on. The 10000 is written as a monetary amount because of *ToString* with the parameter "C" which stands for currency.

The rest of the statements we've already seen before, so there's no need to explain them again.

Below is a list of possibilities for the ToString conversion on strings containing numerical values:

"C" or "c"	Currency
"D" or "d"	Decimal
"E" or "e"	Exponential (scientific)
"F" or "f"	Fixed-point
"G" or "g"	General
"N" or "n"	Number
"P" or "p"	Percent
"R" or "r"	Round-trip
"X" or "x"	Hexadecimal

CHAPTER 10

CALLING EXTERNAL PROGRAMS

Using the Windows Shell

Up to now we have always been working with output to the screen or to a file. What if we want to send output to a printer? Unfortunately to do this from a console app in Visual Basic we need concepts and coding that is very difficult and well outside the scope of this book.

We can, however, write the output to a file in the format that we want the printout to look, and then call an external program like Notepad to open that file and print the contents from there.

To do this I've taken the last program and added code to give the user an option to print to a printer.

Program: Windows Shell – Printing to Printer

```
01  Imports System.IO
02  Namespace PrintToPrinter
03      Public Class Employee
04          Public empNum As Integer
05          Public name As String
06          Public salary As Double
07      End Class
08
09      Public Class PrintingToPrinter
10
```

```
11      Shared Sub Main()
12        Const cEnd As Integer = 999
13        Const delim As String = ","
14        Const fileName As String = "EmployeeData.txt"
15        Const printFlag As Char = "P"
16
17        Dim outFile As StreamWriter
18        Dim emp As New Employee
19        Dim answer As Char = "p"
20
21        SetUpConsole("Read and Write a Sequential File")
22
23        Using FS As New FileStream(fileName, FileMode.Append
24                                          FileAccess.Write)
25          outFile = New StreamWriter(FS)
26
27          Console.Write("Enter employee number or " & cEnd &
28                        " to quit » ")
29          emp.empNum = Convert.ToInt32(Console.ReadLine())
30
31          While (emp.empNum <> cEnd)
32            Console.Write("Enter last name » ")
33            emp.name = Console.ReadLine()
34            Console.Write("Enter salary » ")
35            emp.salary = Convert.ToDouble(Console.ReadLine())
36            outFile.WriteLine(emp.empNum & delim &
37                              emp.name & delim & emp.salary)
38            Console.Write("Enter next employee number or " &
39                          cEnd & " to quit » ")
40            emp.empNum = Convert.ToInt32(Console.ReadLine())
41          End While
42        End Using
43
```

```vbnet
44          Dim reader As StreamReader
45          Dim recordIn As String
46          Dim fields() As String
47
48          Dim PrintHead As New StreamWriter("PrintFile.txt")
49
50          Console.WriteLine(vbCrLf & "{0, -5} {1, -25} {2, 10}",
51                      "Num", "Name", "Salary" & vbCrLf)
52
53          PrintHead.WriteLine("{0, -5} {1, -25} {2, 10}",
54                      "Num", "Name", "Salary")
55          PrintHead.Close()
56
57          Dim PrintStream As New StreamWriter("PrintFile.txt", True)
58
59          Using FS As New FileStream(fileName, FileMode.Open,
60                          FileAccess.Read)
61             reader = New StreamReader(FS)
62             recordIn = reader.ReadLine()
63
64             While recordIn <> ""
65                fields = recordIn.Split(delim)
66                emp.empNum = Convert.ToInt32(fields(0))
67                emp.name = fields(1)
68                emp.salary = Convert.ToDouble(fields(2))
69                Console.WriteLine("{0,-5} {1,-25} {2,10}", emp.empNum,
70                                emp.name, emp.salary.ToString("C"))
71                PrintStream.WriteLine("{0,-5} {1,-25} {2,10}",
72                    emp.empNum, emp.name, emp.salary.ToString("C"))
73                recordIn = reader.ReadLine()
74             End While
75          End Using
76
```

```vb
77      PrintStream.Close()
78
79      Console.WriteLine(vbCrLf & "Press p to print")
80      answer = Char.ToUpper(Console.ReadKey().KeyChar)
81      If answer = printFlag Then
82          Printer()
83      End If
84
85      Console.ReadKey()
86   End Sub
87
88   Shared Sub SetUpConsole(Name As String)
89       Console.Title = Name
90       Console.BackgroundColor = ConsoleColor.White
91       Console.ForegroundColor = ConsoleColor.Black
92       Console.Clear()
93   End Sub
94
95   Shared Sub Printer()
96
97       Dim OpenCMD
98       OpenCMD = CreateObject("wscript.shell")
99       OpenCMD.run("Notepad.exe /p PrintFile.txt")
100     End Sub
101   End Class
102 End Namespace
```

Output 1: Windows Shell – Printing to Printer

```
▣ Read and Write a Sequential File
Enter employee number or 999 to quit » 999

Num    Name                    Salary

123    Van Wyk                 $1,234.56
456    Wessels                 $6,543.21
789    Other                   $9,876.54

Press p to print
```

Printing Contents Shown in Notepad

```
▣ PrintFile.txt - Notepad
File  Edit  Format  View  Help
Num    Name                    Salary
123    Van Wyk                 $1,234.56
456    Wessels                 $6,543.21
789    Other                   $9,876.54
```

Discussion: Windows Shell – Printing to Printer

As usual we're only going to look at new concepts and code.

In line 15, Const printFlag As Char = "P", we create a constant called *printFlag* and initiate it to a capital letter *P*. We are going to use this constant to compare to the input from the console to see if we must print the contents of a file to the printer. The use of a capital letter will be discussed later.

In line 19, Dim answer As Char = "p", we declare a variable as a character type and initiate it to a small letter *p*. We will compare the value of this variable to the flag created in line 15 to find if the print subroutine must be called.

In line 48, Dim PrintHead As New StreamWriter("PrintFile.txt"), we create a streamwriter called *PrintHead* that we're going to use to print the same heading that we're writing to the console, to the file called *PrintFile.txt* on the disk. This file will be used if we want to print the contents of the file to the printer.

In line 53, PrintHead.WriteLine("{0, -5} {1, -25} {2, 10}", and line 54, "Num", "Name", "Salary"), we use the streamwriter *PrintHead*, to write the same values that we wrote to the console, to the file *PrintFile.txt*.

In line 55, PrintHead.Close(), we close the streamwriter. This will flush the contents of the stream to the disk and set the streamwriter up to be used again.

In line 57, Dim **PrintStream** As New StreamWriter("PrintFile.txt", True), we create a streamwriter with the name *PrintStream*, and connect it to the file *PrintFile.txt* to print the contents of the records to our print file. Note the parameter *True*, which will append the values to the end of the file for each write line statement.

In line 71, PrintStream.WriteLine("{0,-5} {1,-25} {2,10}", and line 72, emp.empNum, emp.name, emp.salary.ToString("C")), we use the streamwriter *PrintStream* to write the same contents that we wrote to the console, to the file on disk.

In line 77, PrintStream.Close(), we close the streamwiter to dispose of all of its contents.

In line 79, Console.WriteLine(vbCrLf & "Press p to print"), we added a new prompt to the console to find if the user wants to print the contents we created, to the printer.

In line 80, answer = Char.ToUpper(Console.ReadKey().KeyChar), we assign the character read from the console to the variable *answer*. We use the *KeyChar* property of *ReadKey* to read a character. To make sure that the program will work correctly when the user enters either a small or a capital letter "p", we use the function *Char.ToUpper*, to change the letter read from the console to upper case to compare to the flag we set in line 15.

In line 81, If answer = printFlag Then, line 82, Printer(), and line 83, End If, we compare the value read from the console, to the print flag to find if the file we created must be sent to the printer. If true, we call a subroutine called *Printer*.

In line 95, Shared Sub Printer(), we create the subroutine called in line 82.

In line 97, Dim openCMD, we create a variable called *openCMD*, that will be used in the next two lines. These two lines will contain the nitty gritty of printing to the default printer.

In line 98, openCMD = CreateObject("wscript.shell"), we instantiate an instance of an outside application into the VBscript runtime. Basically, in the case of **wscript.shell**, it creates an object that is an instance of the Windows **shell,** allowing you to run commands against the Windows **shell** from within your VBScript.

We can use *CreateObject* to create new excel applications, word applications, macros, basically any application installed on the machine that has a VBScript API.

In line 99, **openCMD.run("Notepad.exe /p PrintFile.txt"),** we give the command to the Microsoft shell we instantiated in line 98, to run the Notepad.exe program and open the file *PrintFile.txt*. The "/p" is a command line argument to tell Notepad to print the file to the default printer. Note that this parameter ("Notepad.exe /p PrintFile.txt") forms part of the command line and is not part of visual Basic.

In the following Class that forms part of the program in the next section, we'll look at two more examples of using the wscript shell. In the first subroutine we'll open a command line and write the contents of the current directory to a text file on disk. In the second subroutine we'll open Windows Edge and display a website. (In this case the website where you can download the Community version of Visual Studio. This version is free.)

Program Segment: Class WindowsShell

```
149    Class WindowsShell
150        Shared Sub OpenCmd()
151            Dim oShell
152            oShell = CreateObject("WScript.Shell")
```

```
153        oShell.run("cmd /C dir > dir.txt")
154        oShell = Nothing
155    End Sub
156
157    Shared Sub OpenEdge()
158        Dim openCMD
159        openCMD = CreateObject("wscript.shell")
160        openCMD.run("cmd /C start microsoft-edge: " &
161            "https://visualstudio.microsoft.com/vs/community/", 0)
162        openCMD = Nothing
163    End Sub
164 End Class
```

Output: Sub OpenCmd() (Shown in Notepad)

```
dir.txt - Notepad
File  Edit  Format  View  Help
 Volume in drive K is Bad
 Volume Serial Number is 6237-0C6E

 Directory of K:\SSD\VB Book\Programs\ExternalObjects\ExternalObjects\bin\Debug

06-Apr-19  06:40 PM    <DIR>          .
06-Apr-19  06:40 PM    <DIR>          ..
06-Apr-19  06:40 PM                 0 dir.txt
14-Mar-19  02:43 PM            49,143 Example.potx
16-Mar-19  01:05 PM            49,125 Example.pptx
06-Apr-19  06:26 PM            15,360 ExternalObjects.exe
20-Feb-19  02:29 PM               189 ExternalObjects.exe.config
06-Apr-19  06:26 PM            30,208 ExternalObjects.pdb
06-Apr-19  06:26 PM               695 ExternalObjects.xml
29-Jun-17  11:04 PM           135,872 Melancholy abstract design slides.potx
08-Mar-16  11:28 AM           147,200 Microsoft.Web.Administration.dll
03-Feb-19  08:48 PM           189,840 Pitchbook.potx
14-Mar-19  02:51 PM               162 power.bat
14-Mar-19  02:18 PM            34,106 Presentation2.pptx
03-Feb-19  09:46 PM           284,446 PREVIEWTEMPLATE.POTX
03-Feb-19  09:01 PM            95,895 QuizShow.potx
03-Feb-19  08:52 PM         1,241,949 Training.potx
23-May-17  01:57 AM         1,765,568 Welcome to PowerPoint(2).potx
              16 File(s)      4,039,758 bytes
               2 Dir(s)  2,788,398,501,888 bytes free
```

Discussion: Program Segment Class WindowsShell

In line 150, Shared Sub OpenCmd(), we declare the subroutine called *OpenCmd()*, and we end it in line 155, End Sub.

In line 151, Dim oShell, we declare a variable called *oShell*. You will see that we don't specify a type for the variable. It will infer its type from the type of the value we assign to it. These types of variables are called *Variant* types. A *Variant* is a special data type that can contain any kind of data except fixed-length String data.

In line 152, oShell = CreateObject("WScript.Shell"), we use the built in *CreateObject()* function to assign a Windows Shell object to the variable *oShell*.

In line 153, oShell.run("cmd /C dir > dir.txt"), we run the windows shell with certain command line parameters. The command prompt (Dos prompt) *cmd* starts a new instance of the Windows command interpreter. In our case it is called with the /C switch. This switch carries out the command specified by the string following it, and then terminates. Our string "dir > dir.txt" returns the contents of the current directory (dir) and send it (>) to a text file called *dir.txt*. If we did not use the C/ switch the command window would have stayed open and we would have to close it ourselves.

In line 154, oShell = Nothing, we dispose of the entire contents of the shell.

The following is a simple set of the command line switches:

CMD [/A | /U] [/Q] [/D] [/E:ON | /E:OFF] [/F:ON | /F:OFF] [/V:ON | /V:OFF] [[/S] [/C | /K]   string]

/C   Carries out the command specified by string and then terminates
/K   Carries out the command specified by string but remains
/S   Modifies the treatment of string after /C or /K (see below)
/Q   Turns echo off
/D   Disable execution of AutoRun commands from registry (see below)
/A   Causes the output of internal commands to a pipe or file to be ANSI
/U   Causes the output of internal commands to a pipe or file to be Unicode

/T:fg Sets the foreground/background colors (see COLOR /? for more info)

/E:ON Enable command extensions (see below)

/E:OFF Disable command extensions (see below)

/F:ON Enable file and directory name completion characters (see below)

/F:OFF Disable file and directory name completion characters (see below)

/V:ON Enable delayed environment variable expansion using ! as the delimiter. For example, /V:ON would allow !var! to expand the variable var at execution time. The var syntax expands variables at input time, which is quite a different thing when inside of a FOR loop.

/V:OFF Disable delayed environment expansion.

You can get the complete description by opening a cmd prompt from Windows with the switch /?.

Output: Sub OpenEdge()

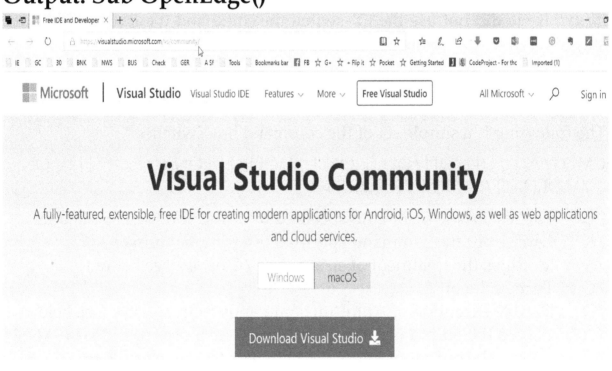

Discussion: Open Edge Example

In the following subroutine we open Windows Edge and display a website as stated before.

In line 157, Shared Sub OpenEdge(), We create a subroutine called *OpenEdge* and end it in line 163.

In line 158, Dim openCMD, we declare a variable of the type Variant with the name of *openCMD*.

In line 159, openCMD = CreateObject("wscript.shell"), we use the built in *CreateObject()* function as befor to assign a Windows Shell object to the variable called *openCMD*.

In line 160, openCMD.run("cmd /C start microsoftedge: " &, and line 161, "https://visualstudio.microsoft.com/vs/community/", 0, True), we use the same command line switch (/C) as in the previous example, but then use the *start* command to start Microsoft Edge. We concatenate the URL of the site we want to open to the previous part of the execution string. Then we supply two parameters that will help to format the execution. The *zero* hides the command window and the *True* forces it to wait for the application to close before continuing. **NB.** It is important to note that not all applications will make use of the last two parameters.

In line 162, openCMD = Nothing, we dispose all of the settings of the shell. Strictly speaking we don't have to do this, but it will asure that we don't run into trouble if we want to use the object again in our code.

USING EXTERNAL OBJECTS

In the following program example we're going to call some external applications and manipulate some of them. **NB.** Here we're not going to use the wscript shell.

In this example we're going to create a small user interface on the console with options that can be chosen by the user.

Program: Using External Objects Example

```
01  Imports System.IO
02  Namespace ExternalObjects
03    Class ExternalObjects
04      Shared Sub Main()
05        Dim iSelection As Integer = 6
06
07        Do While iSelection > 0 And iSelection < 8
08          iSelection = SelectItem()
09          Select Case iSelection
10            Case 1
11              Applications.OpenWord()
12            Case 2
13              Applications.OpenExcel()
14            Case 3
15              WindowsShell.OpenCmd()
16            Case 4
17              WindowsShell.OpenEdge()
18            Case 5
19              Applications.OpenPowerpoint()
20            Case 6
21              Applications.NewPowerpoint()
22            Case 7
23              End
24          End Select
```

```
25
26          If iSelection = 8 Then
27              iSelection = 7
28          End If
29      Loop
30  End Sub
31
32  Shared Function SelectItem() As Integer
33      Dim cSelect As Char
34
35      Console.Clear()
36      SetUpConsole("External Objects")
37
38      Console.WriteLine("Select Option by Pressing the Number" &
39                          vbCrLf)
40      Console.WriteLine("1. Open Word Document")
41      Console.WriteLine("2. Create New Excel Document")
42      Console.WriteLine("3. Create File of Current Directory")
43      Console.WriteLine("4. Open Microsoft Edge")
44      Console.WriteLine("5. Open Existing Powerpoint and " &
45                          "add 3 Blank Slides")
46      Console.WriteLine("6. Open New Powerpoint and " &
47              "add 3 Blank Slides")
48      Console.WriteLine("7. END")
49
50      cSelect = Console.ReadKey().KeyChar()
51
52      If cSelect > "0" And cSelect < "8" Then
53          Return Val(cSelect)
54      Else
55          Console.WriteLine()
56          Console.Write("Invalid Option : Press Return to Continue ")
```

```vbnet
57          Console.ReadKey()
58          Return 8
59      End If
60    End Function
61
62    Shared Sub SetUpConsole(Name As String)
63       Console.Title = Name
64       Console.BackgroundColor = ConsoleColor.Gray
65       Console.ForegroundColor = ConsoleColor.Black
66       Console.Clear()
67    End Sub
68  End Class
69
70  Class Applications
71    Shared Sub OpenWord()
72       Dim WordCMD
73       Dim oDoc
74       Dim oPara
75       WordCMD = CreateObject("Word.Application")
76       Dim curDir = Path.Combine(Environment.CurrentDirectory)
77       If File.Exists(curDir & "/dir.txt") Then
78          WordCMD.Documents.Open(curDir & "/dir.txt")
79       Else
80          oDoc = WordCMD.Documents.Add
81          oPara = oDoc.Content.Paragraphs.Add
82          oPara.Range.Text = "This is a blank file because " &
83                             "the file ""dir.txt"" does not exist."
84          oPara.Range.Font.Name = "Verdana"
85          oPara.Range.Font.Color = 255 'Set color to red
86          oPara.Range.Font.Bold = False
87          oPara.range.Font.Size = 24
88          oPara.Format.SpaceAfter = 6    '6 pt spacing after paragraph.
89          oPara.Range.InsertParagraphAfter()
90       End If
```

```vb
91        WordCMD.Visible = True
92     End Sub
93
94     Shared Sub OpenExcel()
95        Dim xlApp
96        Dim xlBook
97        Dim xlSheet
98        xlApp = CreateObject("Excel.Application")
99        xlBook = xlApp.Workbooks.Add
100       xlSheet = xlBook.Worksheets(1)
101       xlSheet.Application.Cells(1, 1).Value = "This is row 1,  column A"
102       xlSheet.Application.Cells(1, 2).Value = "This is row 1,  column B"
103       xlSheet.Application.Cells(2, 1).Value = "This is row 2,  column A"
104       xlSheet.Application.Cells(2, 2).Value = "This is row 2,  column B"
105       xlSheet.Columns.AutoFit()
106       xlApp.visible = True
107    End Sub
108
109    Shared Sub OpenPowerpoint()
110       Dim pptApp
111       Dim activePresentation
112       Dim pptSlide
113       Dim pptLayout
114       Dim curDir = Path.Combine(Environment.CurrentDirectory)
115
116       pptApp = CreateObject("Powerpoint.Application")
117       activePresentation = pptApp.Presentations.open(curDir &
118                        "\Example.pptx")
119       pptLayout = activePresentation.SlideMaster.CustomLayouts(4)
120       pptSlide = activePresentation.slides.AddSlide(
121               activePresentation.slides.count + 1, pptLayout)
122       pptSlide = activePresentation.Slides.AddSlide(
123               activePresentation.slides.count + 1, pptLayout)
```

```
124        pptSlide = activePresentation.Slides.AddSlide(
125                    activePresentation.slides.count + 1, pptLayout)
126        pptApp.visible = True
127     End Sub
128
129     Shared Sub NewPowerpoint()
130        Dim pptApp
131        Dim activePresentation
132        Dim pptSlide
133        Dim pptLayout
134        Dim curDir = Path.Combine(Environment.CurrentDirectory)
135
136        pptApp = CreateObject("Powerpoint.Application")
137        activePresentation = pptApp.Presentations.add
138        pptLayout = activePresentation.SlideMaster.CustomLayouts(7)
139        pptSlide = activePresentation.slides.AddSlide(
140                    activePresentation.slides.count + 1, pptLayout)
141        pptSlide = activePresentation.Slides.AddSlide(
142                    activePresentation.slides.count + 1, pptLayout)
143        pptSlide = activePresentation.Slides.AddSlide(
144                    activePresentation.slides.count + 1, pptLayout)
145        pptApp.visible = True
146     End Sub
147  End Class
148
149  Class WindowsShell
150    Shared Sub OpenCmd()
151        Dim oShell
152        oShell = CreateObject("WScript.Shell")
153        oShell.run("cmd /C dir > dir.txt")
154        oShell = Nothing
155    End Sub
156
```

```
157    Shared Sub OpenEdge()
158        Dim openCMD
159        openCMD = CreateObject("wscript.shell")
160        openCMD.run("cmd /C start microsoft-edge: " &
161              "https://visualstudio.microsoft.com/vs/community/", 0)
162        openCMD = Nothing
163      End Sub
164   End Class
165 End Namespace
```

Output: The Interface

```
External Objects

Select Option by Pressing the Number

1. Open Word Document
2. Create New Excel Document
3. Create File of Current Directory
4. Open Microsoft Edge
5. Open Existing Powerpoint and add 3 Blank Slides
6. Open New Powerpoint and add 3 Blank Slides
7. END
```

Discussion: The Interface

In line 5, Dim iSelection As Integer = 6, we create a flag that we'll use to see which option the user selected. As you see in the interface, valid options are from 1 to 7. The variable is initiated with the value 6 (it could actually have been any value from 1 to 7) to force the loop in lines 7 to 29 to execute at least once in order for the console, as shown above, to be created.

In line 7, Do While iSelection > 0 And iSelection < 8, we create the loop that will keep iterating until the option 7 is chosen to end the program. As you can see we have used a combined condition that consists of two conditions connected with the comparison operator *And*. In this case **both** the conditions must be **true** for the while loop to carry on iterating.

For Boolean comparison of the *And* operator, the result is True only if both expression 1, and expression2 evaluate to True. The following table illustrates how the result is determined.

Table.

If expression1 is	And expression2 is	The value of result is
True	True	True
True	False	False
False	True	False
False	False	False

In a Boolean comparison, the *And* operator always evaluates both expressions, which could include making procedure calls. In case the first condition is false the second condition will still be checked, even when the combined condition can never be true.

The *AndAlso* operator performs short-circuiting, which means that if expression1 is False, then expression2 is not evaluated.

In line 8, iSlection = SelectItem(), we assign the value that is returned by the function *SelectItem()* to the variable *iSelection*.

The code in lines 9 to 24 makes use of the *Select Case* statement which is also a selection statement.

Syntax for the select case statement

Select [Case] testexpression
   [Case expressionlist
     [statements]]
   [Case Else
     [elsestatements]]
End Select

In line 9, Select Case selection, we set up the condition to be evaluated by the select case statement. The value of the variable *iSelection* is compared to each of the *Case* options in lines 10, 12, 14, 16, 18, 20, and 22, using short-circuit evaluation.

Don't be confused by the fact that the operands are numbered 1 to 7. It is not the number of the case statement, but the value of the condition that will be compared to the value of the variable *iSelection*. In our case it is numerical values, but it can be of any type.

In line 10, Case 1, we compare the value in the variable called *iSelection* to the value *1* specified by the *Case* statement. If the result returns *True* the statement in the next line, line 11, Applications.OpenWord(), will be executed. In this case the *OpenWord()* method of the class *Applications* will be called. After that method is completed controll will be passed back to the select case statement and jump to the *End Select* statement.

The same explanation is applicable to the rest of the cases except the case in line 22. In this case the statement in line 23, End, will be executed. All resources used in the program will be disposed of, and the execution stopped.

In line 24, End Select, the selection structure is ended.

In some cases it is necessary to include a *Case Else* statement to be executed when none of the cases evaluates to true.

In line 26, If iSelection = 8 Then, line 27, iSelection = 7, and line 28, End If, we use an if statement to catch a case where an invalid value has been returned by the *SelectItem()* function. We could have used any valid value (any number from 1 to 7) in line 27 to force the loop to be executed one more time.

In line 32, Shared Function SelectItem() As Integer, we declare a function called *SelectItem* of the type integer. In this function we show the user interface on the console and capture the option entered by the user. Most of the code here you know already and we'll not look at it again.

In line 33, Dim cSelect As Char, we declare a variable called *cSelect* of the type *char*, which you will remember, can contain one alphanumeric character.

In line 50, cSelect = Console.ReadKey().KeyChar(), we read one character from the console and assign the value to the variable *cSelect*. This variable contains the option entered by the user.

In line 52, If cSelect > "0" And cSelect < "8" Then, an if statement is started to see if the value entered by the user in line 50 is valid. The valid options are 1 to 7. Remember that *cSelect* can only contain alphanumeric values, that's why we have the quotation marks around the values in the if statement. We also use the *And* operator as we did previously.

If the condition in line 52 evaluates to *True*, controll is passed to line 53, Return Val(cSelect), where we return the numeric value of the *Char* type variable *cSelect* to the caller.

If the condition in line 52 evaluates to *False*, line 53 is skipped and controll passes on to the *Else* statement in line 54. Here we display a message on the console to tell the user that an invalid option was taken, and carry on to the next line.

In line 58, Return 8, we return the value 8 to the caller. Remember we checked in the main subroutine (line 26) for this value. You will see that we return the numeric value 8 and not the alphanumeric value "8". We do this because the function had been declared as integer.

At this stage we have created the console shown in the **Output** image and must react on the input we received. Done in *Sub Main*.

Discussion: Word Example

In line 70, Class Applications, we declare a class called *Applications*.

In line 71, Shared Sub OpenWord(), we create the subroutine called *OpenWord()*. In this subroutine we will try to open a file with MS Word. If the file exists MS Word will open it, but if it doesn't exist we will open a new doc, and add some text to it.

In line 72, Dim WordCMD, we create a variable of the type *variant*, that will connect to an instance of MS Word.

In line 73, Dim oDoc, we create a variable of the type *variant*, that will connect to an instance of a document in MS Word.

In line 74, Dim oPara, we create a variable of the type *variant*, that will connect to an instance of a paragraph object in MS Word.

In line 75, WordCMD = CreateObject("Word.Application"), we use the *CreateObject* function to assign a Word Application to the variable *WordCMD*. The variant variable takes the type from the function and thus have an Object type.

In line 76, Dim curDir = Path.Combine(Environment.CurrentDirectory), we create a variable called *curDir* to store the full path and name of the current directory.

The *Path Class* performs operations on string instances that contain file or directory path information.

The *Combine* method of the *Path* class combines strings into a path. The path can be either absolute or relative. An absolute path starts at the root directory like c:\abc\def\, while the relative path starts with the directory in relation to the current position. This is what we did in some of our previous programs where we specified only the file name, with the result that it used the current directory of the executable program. In other words the location where the *exe* file of the program resides.

The *Environment Class* retrieves information about directories and logical drives.

The *CurrentDirectory* method of the environment class returns the absolute path of the directory where the executable program resides.

In line 77, If File.Exists(curDir & "/dir.txt") Then, we use the *Exists* method of the *File* class to find if the file in the parameter exists. In our case the path is stored in the *curDir* variable and the name of the file is the literal value concatenated to the value in the variable. So, we're checking to see if the file *dir.txt* exists in the current directory. Note that we concatenated the forward slash in front of the file name because the current directory does not include the slash in the path. If the file exists, control goes to the next line (78). If not, it carries on with line 80.

In line 78, WordCMD.Documents.Open(curDir & "/dir.txt"), the *Open* method of the *Documents* collection opens the existing Microsoft Office Word document specified by our fully qualified path and file name (curDir & "/dir.txt"). This method returns a document that is represented in our object variable called *WordCMD*.

In line 80, oDoc = WordCMD.Documents.Add, that receives control when the file does not exist, we use the *Add* method to add a new document to the Documents collection of the object *WordCMD*. This document is represented by the *oDoc* variable.

In line 81, oPara = oDoc.Content.Paragraphs.Add, we use the *Add* method to add a new paragraph to the *Paragraphs* collection of the contents of the *oDoc* object we created in line 80. This paragraph is represented by the *oPara* variable.

In line 82, oPara.Range.Text = "This is a blank file because " &, and line 83, "the file ""dir.txt"" does not exist.", we use *Range.Text* to set the contents of the *range* represented by the object *oPara*. The *Range.Text* method returns or sets the text in the specified range or selection; *oPara* in our case. Note the double quotation marks around *dir.txt*. We have to use double quotation marks to enter the quotation marks in the string. Single quotation marks will result in a syntax error.

In line 84, oPara.Range.Font.Name = "Verdana", we use the *Name* property of the *Font* collection to set the *Font* of our range (oPara) to *Verdana*.

In line 85, oPara.Range.Font.Color = 255, we set the font color of *oPara* to **red**. Unfortunately the VB constants cannot be used here.

In line 86, oPara.Range.Font.Bold = False, we set the *Bold* property of the font in our paragraph to *False* to turn it off.

In line 87, oPara.range.Font.Size = 24, we set the size of the font in our paragraph to 24 points.

In line 88, oPara.Format.SpaceAfter = 6, we set the format of our paragraph to add 6 points after the paragraph.

In line 89, oPara.Range.InsertParagraphAfter(), we insert a paragraph after our paragraph, by using the *InsertParagraphAfter()* method.

In line 91, WordCMD.Visible = True, we set the *Visible* property of our *WordCMD* object to true, so we can see it, and give it the focus.

Output: Word - When File Exists

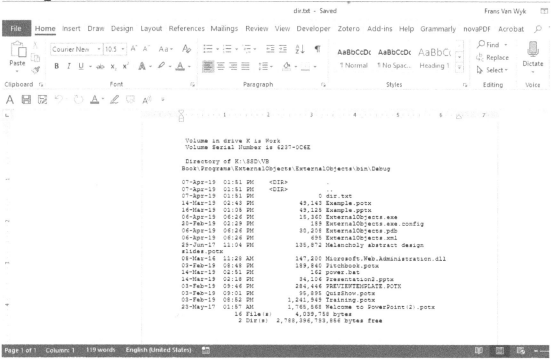

Output: Word - When File Does Not Exist

Discussion: Excel Example

In line 94, Shared Sub OpenExcel(), we declare a subroutine called *OpenExcel()*. In this subroutine we will create a new Excel spreadsheet consisting of one workbook and one worksheet with some data added.

In line 95, Dim xlApp, we create an object variable to contain the *Excel App*.

In line 96, Dim xlBook, we create an object variable to contain the *Excel Workbook*.

In line 97, Dim xlSheet, we create an object variable to contain the *Excel Spreadsheet*.

In line 98, xlApp = CreateObject("Excel.Application"), we use the *CreateObject* function to assign an Excel Application to the variable *xlApp*. The variant variable takes its type from the function and thus have an Object type.

In line 99, xlBook = xlApp.Workbooks.Add, we use the *Add* method to add a new workbook to the Workbooks collection of the object *xlApp*. This workbook is represented by the *xlBook* variable.

In line 100, xlSheet = xlBook.Worksheets(1), we connect the first *Worksheet* in the *Worksheets collection* to the variable *xlSheet*.

In line 101, xlSheet.Application.Cells(1, 1).Value = "This is row 1, column A", we set the *Value* of the specified *cell (1,1)* of the *cells collection* in the *Worksheet* referred to by the variable *xlSheet*. The numbering of the cells is the same as for a table; the row first then the column. In this case the value of the cell in row one column one is set to the literal value *This is row 1, column A*.

The same explanation as above applies to the following three lines where only the cell numbering and the literal values differ:

102, xlSheet.Application.Cells(1, 2).Value = "This is row 1, column B",
103, xlSheet.Application.Cells(2, 1).Value = "This is row 2, column A", and
104, xlSheet.Application.Cells(2, 2).Value = "This is row 2, column B".

In line 105, xlSheet.Columns.AutoFit(), we set the *AutoFit* property of all the columns in the worksheet, with the result that the columns fit the contents of each cell in that specific column.

In line 106, xlApp.visible = True, we make the *Excel Application* visible and set the focus to it.

Output: Excel Example

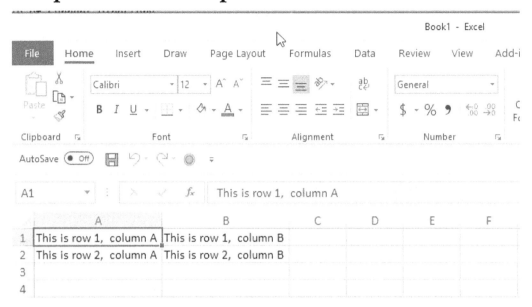

Discussion: Powerpoint Example

In line 109, Shared Sub OpenPowerpoint(), we declare the subroutine called *OpenPowerpoint*. In this subroutine we will open an existing Powerpoint presentation and add some empty slides to it. Remember that the presentation must be available in the current directory where the program will execute.

In line 110 to 113 we created variables for the application, the active presentation, the slide, and the layout.

Line 114, Dim curDir = Path.Combine(Environment.CurrentDirectory), sets up the current directory.

Line 116 sets up *pptApp* to contain a Powerpoint presentation.

Line 117, activePresentation = pptApp.Presentations.open(curDir &, and line 118, "\Example.pptx"), opens the Powerpoint file called *Example.pptx* and connects it to *activePresentation*. Example.pptx must reside in the same directory as the executable program.

In line 119, pptLayout = activePresentation.SlideMaster.CustomLayouts(1), we use the *CustomLayouts* property of the *SlideMaster* object to return a *CustomLayouts* collection. We use *CustomLayouts* (INDEX), where index is the custom layout index number, to return a single *CustomLayout* object. In our case the index is 1.

In line 120, pptSlide = activePresentation.slides.AddSlide, and line 121, activePresentation.slides.count + 1, pptLayout, we use the *AddSlide* method to add a new slide to the *slides* collection of the active presentation. We add the new slide to the first position after the last slide in the collection (slides.count +1). The variable *pptLayout* which we set up in line 119 is used to represent the layout of the slide we added.

Line 122 to125 uses the same syntax to add another two slides with the same layout. So we will end up with three similar slides at the end of the presentation.

In line 126, pptApp.visible = True, we make the app visible and set the focus to it.

Output: Example.pptx before slides are added

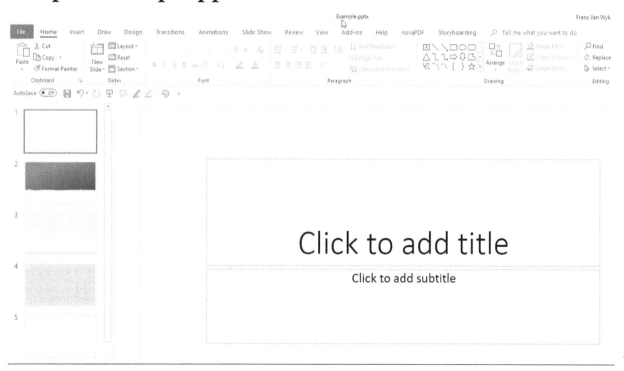

Output: Example.pptx after slides are added

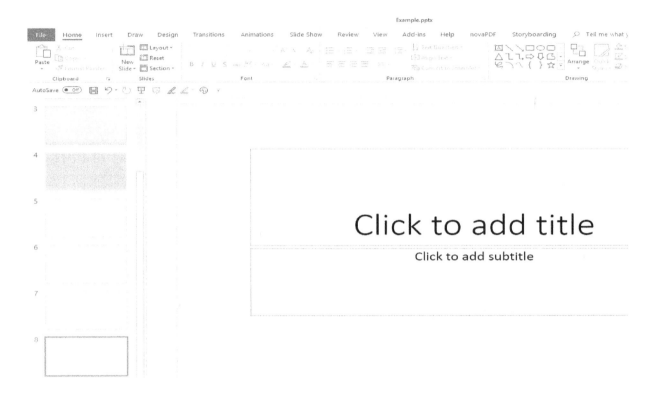

In line 129, Shared Sub NewPowerpoint(), we declare a new subroutine called *NewPowerpoint()*. In this subroutine we will create a new Powerpoint presentation and add three blank slides to it.

The rest of the lines are the same as before with two exceptions. The first is in line 137 where we just add a presentation to the active presentation and don't open an existing presentation first, and the second exeption is that we use *CustomLayouts* with index 7 and not 1. This layout uses a totally blank slide.

Output: Blank Powerpoint Example

Visual Studio IDE

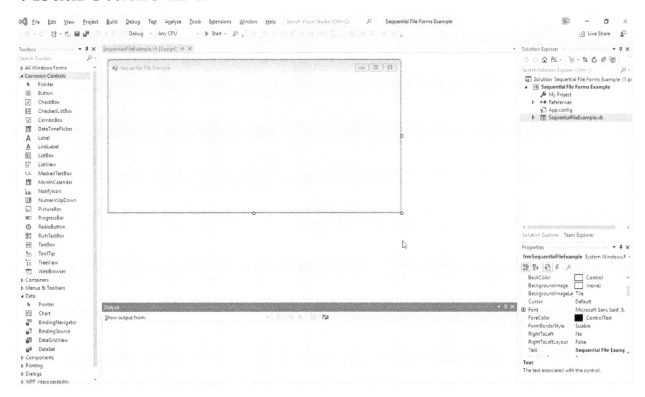

CHAPTER 11

FORMS APPLICATIONS

Introduction

Up to now we chose to create a console App in Visual Studio.

You know by now that we even had to create the user interface by means of code, like we did in the last programming example. I used that option specifically because I wanted to explain the coding principles, and I hoped you would download Visual Studio and work with me.

The other main option we have is to open a Windows Forms App in Visual Studio.

A Windows Forms application is built on classes from the **Windows.Forms** namespace that forms part of the **System** Namespace.

In Windows Forms, a *form* is a visual interface on which you display information to the user. You normally build Windows Forms applications by placing controls on forms. You then develop responses to actions, such as mouse clicks or key presses, by the user.

A *control* is an individually distinct user interface (UI) element that displays data or accepts data input.

When a user does something to your form or one of its controls, it generates an *event*. Your application reacts to these events by using code, and processes the events when they occur.

List of Common Controls

Windows Forms contains a number of controls that you can place on forms. These controls vary, and can display text boxes, buttons, drop-down boxes, radio buttons, and even Web pages.

▲ Common Controls
- ↖ Pointer
- [ab] Button
- ☑ CheckBox
- ☰ CheckedListBox
- 🖹 ComboBox
- 📅 DateTimePicker
- A Label
- A LinkLabel
- 📇 ListBox
- ⠿ ListView
- (.). MaskedTextBox
- 📅 MonthCalendar
- ⌐ NotifyIcon
- 🔢 NumericUpDown
- 🖼 PictureBox
- ▭ ProgressBar
- ◉ RadioButton
- 🖹 RichTextBox
- [ab] TextBox
- 🖹 ToolTip
- ⦂ TreeView
- 🖥 WebBrowser

Button Control

Presents a standard button that the user can click to perform actions.

CheckBox Control

Indicates whether a condition is on or off.

CheckedListBox Control

Displays a list of items with a check box next to each item.

ComboBox Control

Displays data in a drop-down combo box.

DateTimePicker Control

Allows the user to select a single item from a list of dates or times.

Label Control

Displays text that cannot be edited by the user.

LinkLabel Control

Allows you to add Web-style links to Windows Forms applications.

ListBox Control

Allows the user to select one or more items from a predefined list.

ListView Control

Displays a list of items with icons, in the manner of Windows Explorer.

MaskedTextBox Control

Constrains the format of user input in a form.

MonthCalendar Control

Presents an intuitive graphical interface for users to view and set date information.

NotifyIcon Component

Displays icons for processes that run in the background and would not otherwise have user interfaces.

NumericUpDown Control

Displays numerals that a user can browse through and select from.

PictureBox Control

Displays graphics in bitmap, GIF, JPEG, metafile, or icon format.

ProgressBar Control

Graphically indicates the progress of an action towards completion.

RadioButton Control

Presents a set of two or more mutually exclusive options to the user.

RichTextBox Control

Allows users to enter, display, and manipulate text with formatting.

TextBox Control

Allows editable, multiline input from the user.

ToolTip Component

Displays text when the user points at other controls.

TreeView Control

Displays a hierarchy of nodes that can be expanded or collapsed, as seen in Windows Explorer.

WebBrowser Control

Hosts Web pages and provides Internet Web browsing capabilities to your application.

Example of a Form With Most Common Controls

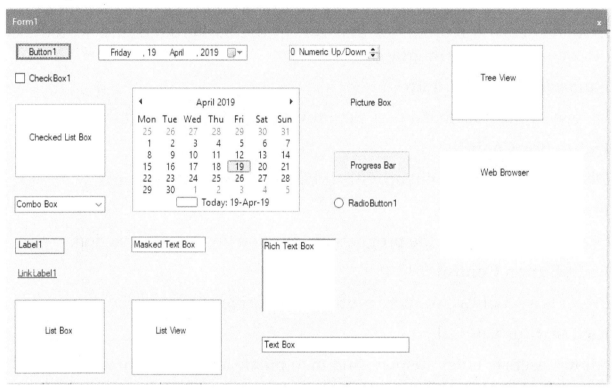

With the Visual Studio drag-and-drop *Windows Forms Designer*, you can easily create Windows Forms applications. Just select the controls with your mouse and add them where you want on the form. The designer provides tools such as gridlines and snap lines to take the hassle out of aligning controls.

There are many other features in Windows Forms that make implementing common tasks such as support for creating dialogboxes, printing, adding Help and documentation, and localizing your application to multiple languages, fast and easy.

Windows Forms incorporates the strong security system of the .NET Framework. This system enables you to supply more secure applications to your customers.

There are quite a few more controls available such as Containers, Menus & Toolbars, Components, Printing, and Dialogs. It is beyond the scope of this book to look at them all.

Now let us see this in action.

You will recognise the example as soon as you see the code.

We start by going through the steps as shown in Chapter 9, but choose the Forms option as discussed above, and choose *Desktop* for *Project Type*.

In our example I named the Project as *Sequential File Forms Example*.

It opened with a Form called *Form1* as you can see on the next page.

On this form we'll be building the user interface for our program. Here's a rough draft on paper.

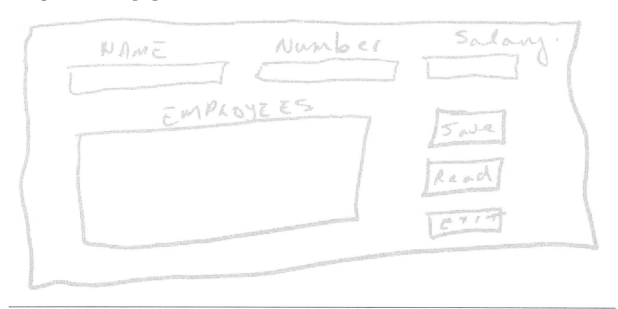

The *Text* property is the text that appears at the top of the form. In our case I changed it to *Sequential File Example* as seen on the right below. To get to

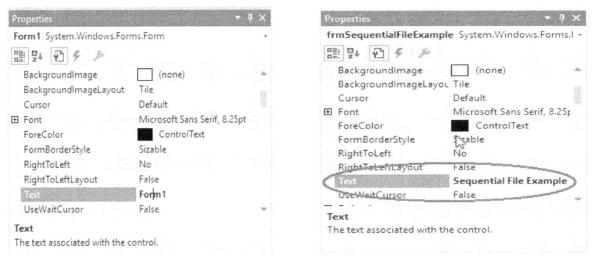

the properties you just click on the form once and then the properties section will be selected.

Next we change the *Name* property of the form from Form1 to *frmSequentialFileExample*. You'll see that a prefix *frm* was added to the form name. It is always a good practice to show what we're working with as part of the objects name for easy reference. See below.

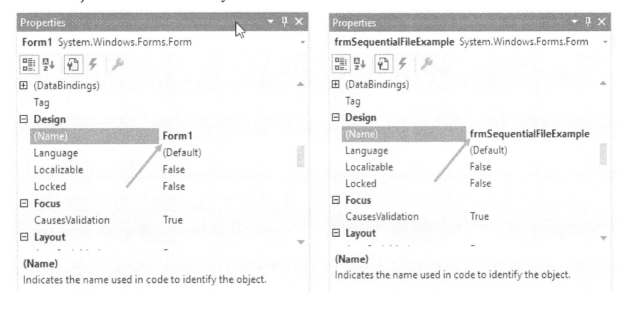

This is what our form looks like now.

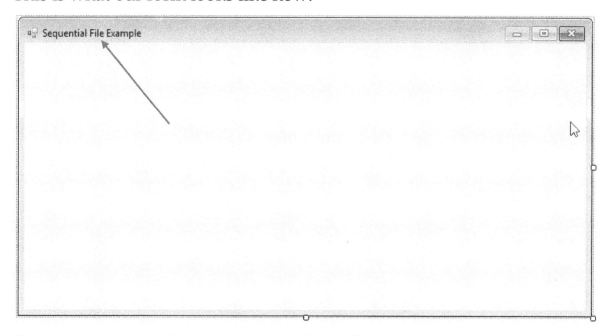

The next step is to place some controls on the form.

We need 4 labels for the headings, 3 text boxes (one each for name, number and salary), 1 list box to display the data, and 3 buttons (one each for save, read and exit).

To get the controls we go to the Toolbox that you saw at the start of this chapter. To place a control on the form we can either press the left mouse button on the control, keep it depressed, and drag the control onto the form, or we can double click on the control. It roughly looks like this.

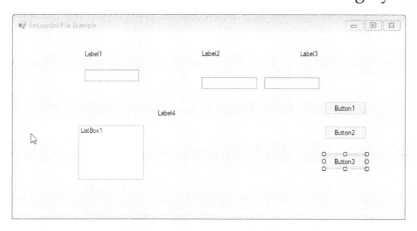

Obviously, we must do some work on this. After the layout is complete it looks like this.

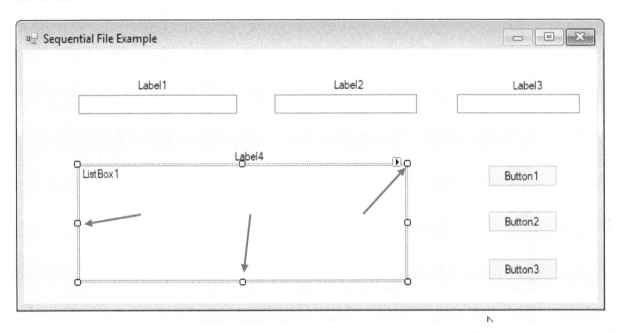

When you click once on a control you will see some handles on the control which you can use to draw the control to the size you want. Just left click on the handle, keep the button depressed, and move the mouse to get the shape you want.

We can now go and set the properties for each of our controls. Left click on a control once and the properties window for that control will be shown as below.

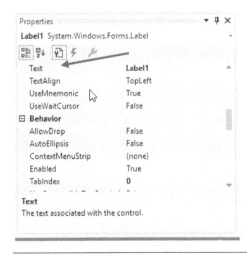

You will see that each of the controls on our form, except the list box have a *Text* property. That is the text that will be displayed on the control. We can now change it appropriately for the labels and the buttons.

Our Form now looks like this.

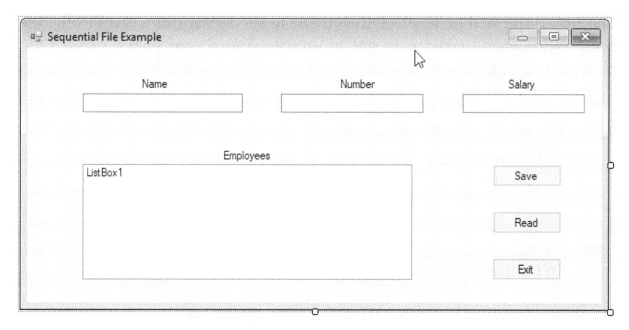

The list box displays its name *ListBox1*, but don't worry about it. The name will disappear when we run our program.

The next step will be to name our controls with appropriate names. When you have the properties menu you can scroll until you find the *Name* property and change the value. Remember to give it meaningful names and use appropriate prefixes. I named the controls in the example *lblName*, *lblNumber*, *lblSalary*, *lblEmployees*, *txtName*, *txtNumber*, *txtSalary*, *btnSave*, *btnRead*, *btnExit*, and *lstBox*.

Obviously, the form will still look the same as we didn't change anything that is displayed.

Now we can start adding code to our program to give it functionality. To do this we're using the *Solution Explorer*.

Right click on the line ▷ ▤ SequentialFileExample.vb and click on *View Code*. The following will show.

Now we can start adding code for our *frmSequentialFileExample* class.

The first thing will be to place the cursor to the left of the word Public, and press enter once or twice to get an empty line above *Public Class*. Enter Imports System.IO

The rest of the code is entered in the class.

```
Public Class frmSequentialFileExample
    Const delim As String = ","
    Const fileName As String = "EmployeeData.txt"
    Public emp As New Employee


    Sub Save()
        Dim Outfile As StreamWriter

        Using FS As New FileStream(fileName, FileMode.Append,
                    FileAccess.Write)
        Outfile = New StreamWriter(FS)

            emp.empNum = Convert.ToInt32(txtNumber.Text)
            emp.name = txtName.Text
            emp.salary = Convert.ToDouble(txtSalary.Text)
            Outfile.WriteLine(emp.empNum & delim & emp.name &
                            delim & emp.salary)
            Outfile.Flush()
        End Using
    End Sub


    Sub Read()
        Dim reader As StreamReader
        Dim recordIn As String
        Dim fields() As String
        lstBox.Items.Add(String.Format("{0,-5} {1,-12} {2, -10}", "Num",
                        "Name", "Salary"))
```

```vb
            Using FS As New FileStream(fileName, FileMode.Open,
                                        FileAccess.Read)
        reader = New StreamReader(FS)
        recordIn = reader.ReadLine()
        Dim lstIndex As Integer = 0
        While recordIn <> ""
            fields = recordIn.Split(delim)
            emp.empNum = Convert.ToInt32(fields(0))
            emp.name = fields(1)
            emp.salary = Convert.ToDouble(fields(2))
            lstBox.Items.Add(String.Format("{0,-5} {1,-12} {2, 10}",
                    emp.empNum, emp.name,  emp.salary.ToString("C")))
            recordIn = reader.ReadLine()
        End While
    End Using
  End Sub
End Class
```

There is still a bit of our project missing. An *Employee* class and code for the three buttons.

To add a class to the project, go to *Project* on the menu and click *Add Class*, and name the class *Employee*.

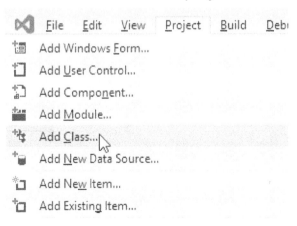

This is what you will get.

```
1 reference
Public Class Employee


End Class
```

In the Class we add the code:

```
Public empNum As Integer
Public name As String
Public salary As Double
```

Insert code in buttons.

To get to the place to insert code for the buttons we double click on each of our buttons on the form.

For the *Save Button* we will get this:

```
Private Sub btnSave_Click(sender As Object, e As EventArgs)
                            Handles btnSave.Click
End Sub
```

This is a subroutine that raises an event when the button is clicked. We add the next code in this subroutine.

```
Save()
txtName.Text = ""
txtNumber.Text = ""
txtSalary.Text = ""
txtName.Select()
```

The first statement calls the subroutine called *Save*, that we created with our code. The next three statements clear the text boxes, and the last statement uses the *Select* event of the text box to place control on the first character of the text box called *txtName*.

In the *Click Event* for the Read button we add *Read()* to call the Read() subroutine we created.

In the *Click Event* for the Exit button we add the statement End that will end execution of the program.

When we run the program we get the form that we created. Here it is shown with the data for the first employee added in the *Text Boxes*.

When we click on the save button this information will be saved in the file *EmployeeData.txt* according to the code in the *Save()* Subroutine.

I'll enter the data for the next two records and then we will click on the *Read* button and see what happens.

The result looks like this.

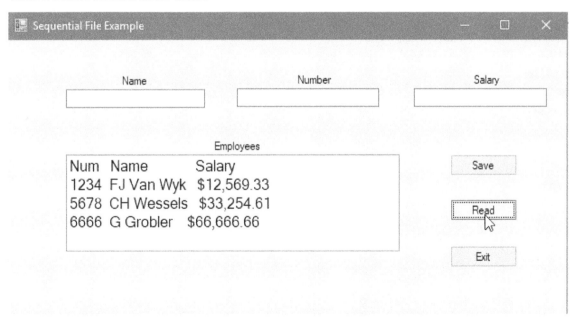

You see that the information for the employees now appears in the list box.

Fine, but why is the Salary value for the last employee not in line with the salary of the other two. This is one of those instances where we will probably think the problem lies in our code, but it actually doesn't. The problem is with the Font type specified for the list box. The font that is the default for the list box is *Microsoft Sans Serif, 8.25pt*. This is a *variable-width font*, where the letters and spacings have different widths to let it look neater when reading. It is just pure luck that the first two lines in our output display correctly.

We can fix our problem by changing the font for the list box to a *monospaced font* (also called a fixed-pitch, fixed-width), or *non-proportional font*, whose letters and characters each occupy the same amount of horizontal space. So let us try the default font for the **code** in our program. This font is called *Consolas*. We have to left click once on the list box and then look for the font property in the list. When we click on the Ellips (…) next to the font we will get a popup screen where we have to look for Consolas and change its properties to what we want.

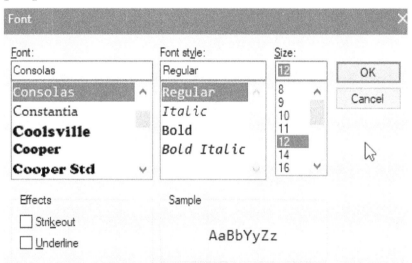

When we run the program now the list box will display correctly.

```
                   Employees

Num    Name          Salary
1234   FJ Van Wyk    $12,569.33
5678   CH Wessels    $33,254.61
6666   G Grobler     $66,666.66
```

You will remember I said the code will seem familiar. The bulk of this code is precisely the same as for our previous Example *Read Write Sequential File*.

The *Employee* class is identical.

I will mark the identical code in the following:

```vb
Imports System.IO
Public Class frmSequentialFileExample
    Const delim As String = ","
    Const fileName As String = "EmployeeData.txt"
    Dim emp As New Employee

    Sub Save()
        Dim Outfile As StreamWriter

        Using FS As New FileStream(fileName, FileMode.Append,
                                FileAccess.Write)
            Outfile = New StreamWriter(FS)

            emp.empNum = Convert.ToInt32(txtNumber.Text)
            emp.name = txtName.Text
            emp.salary = Convert.ToDouble(txtSalary.Text)
            Outfile.WriteLine(emp.empNum & delim & emp.name &
                            delim & emp.salary)
            Outfile.Flush()
        End Using
    End Sub
    Sub Read()
        Dim reader As StreamReader
        Dim recordIn As String
        Dim fields() As String
        Using FS As New FileStream(fileName, FileMode.Open,
                                FileAccess.Read)
```

```vb
        reader = New StreamReader(FS)
        recordIn = reader.ReadLine()
        Dim lstIndex As Integer = 0
        lstBox.Items.Add(String.Format("{0,-5} {1,-12} {2, -10}", "Num",
                                       "Name", "Salary"))
        While recordIn <> ""
            fields = recordIn.Split(delim)
            emp.empNum = Convert.ToInt32(fields(0))
            emp.name = fields(1)
            emp.salary = Convert.ToDouble(fields(2))
            lstBox.Items.Add(String.Format("{0,-5} {1,-12} {2, 10}",
                    emp.empNum, emp.name, emp.salary.ToString("C")))
            recordIn = reader.ReadLine()
        End While
    End Using
End Sub

Private Sub BtnSave_Click(sender As Object, e As EventArgs) Handles
                          btnSave.Click
    Save()
    txtName.Text = ""
    txtNumber.Text = ""
    txtSalary.Text = ""
    txtName.Select()
End Sub

Private Sub BtnRead_Click(sender As Object, e As EventArgs) Handles
                          btnRead.Click
    Read()
End Sub

Private Sub BtnExit_Click(sender As Object, e As EventArgs) Handles
                          btnExit.Click
    End
End Sub
End Class
```

The unmarked code.

In the *Save()* subroutine we assign the values in the text boxes where we entered the data to the properties of the *Employee Class*.

We use the statement, Outfile.Flush(), to write the data to the file on disk.

In the *Read()* subroutine we use the statement, Dim lstIndex As Integer = 0, to set the starting point to the first line in the list box. (Remember the index starts at zero)

The statement, lstBox.Items.Add(String.Format("{0,-5} {1,-12} {2,-10}", "Num", "Name", "Salary")) adds a string representing the header to the index position of the list box. In our case the first line in the list box, because we set the value to zero in the declaration.

In the loop we use the statement, lstBox.Items.Add(String.Format("{0,-5} {1,-12} {2, 10}", emp.empNum, emp.name, emp.salary.ToString("C"))) to add each line we read from the file to the next line in the list box.

The statement, Private Sub BtnSave_Click(sender As Object, e As EventArgs) Handles btnSave.Click, calls the subroutine when its button is clicked.

The statement, Save(), calls the *Save()* subroutine we declared in the code.

The statements, txtName.Text = "", txtNumber.Text = "", and txtSalary.Text = "" Clears the three text boxes for new data to be entered.

The statement, txtName.Select(), selects the text box called *txtName* and places the cursor on the first character in the text box.

The statement, Private Sub BtnRead_Click(sender As Object, e As EventArgs) Handles btnRead.Click, calls the subroutine when its button is clicked.

The statement, Read(), calls the *Read()* subroutine we declared in the code.

The statement, Private Sub BtnExit_Click(sender As Object, e As EventArgs) Handles btnExit.Click, calls the subroutine when its button is clicked.

The statement, End, stops the execution of the program.

TEXT TO SPEECH FORMS EXAMPLE

To show you how easy it is to do something really cool, I've included this example.

The interface looks like this:

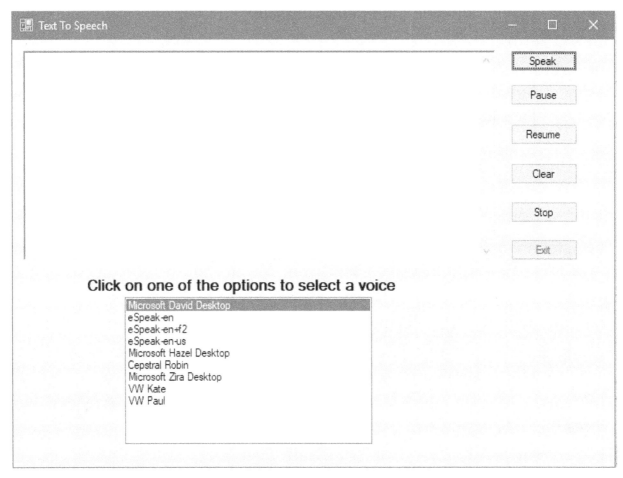

Before we look at the code let's see what this program does.

It has a big *RichTextBox* where we can place text to be changed to speech. We can click anywhere on the text box and press ctrl+v to paste text from the clipboard into the text box. Alternatively, we can right click anywhere in the text box. We will then be asked if we want to paste the clipboard contents into the text box.

As you will see we can then click on either the *Yes* or the *No* button with obvious results.

As you can see on the form, we have a *ListBox* showing the voices on our computer that we can choose from. If we do nothing it will use the default voice, else it will use the voice we selected.

The *Command Buttons* executes the obvious actions. Starts reading, pause reading, resume reading, stops reading, clears the text box, and stops execution of the program.

Program: Text to Speech Example.

```
01    Imports System.Speech
02    Imports System.Speech.Synthesis
03    Public Class frmTextToSpeach
04        Dim reader As New SpeechSynthesizer
05
06        Private Sub btnSpeak_Click(sender As Object, e As EventArgs)
07                                  Handles   btnSpeak.Click
08        If RichTextBox1.Text <> "" Then
09            reader.Dispose()
10            reader = New SpeechSynthesizer
11            reader.SelectVoice(lstboxVoices.Text)
12            reader.SpeakAsync(RichTextBox1.Text)
13        Else
14            MessageBox.Show("Pease enter text")
15        End If
16        End Sub
```

```vb
17      Private Sub btnPause_Click(sender As Object, e As EventArgs)
18                              Handles btnPause.Click
19          If reader IsNot Nothing Then
20              If reader.State = SynthesizerState.Speaking Then
21                  reader.Pause()
22              End If
23          End If
24      End Sub
25
26      Private Sub Form1_Load(sender As Object, e As EventArgs) Handles
27                              MyBase.Load
28          Dim lstVoices As New List(Of String)()
29          Dim synth As New SpeechSynthesizer
30
31          For Each voice In synth.GetInstalledVoices
32              lstVoices.Add(voice.VoiceInfo.Name)
33          Next
34
35          For Each child In lstVoices
36              lstboxVoices.Items.Add(child)
37          Next
38          lstboxVoices.SetSelected(0, True)
39      End Sub
40
41      Private Sub btnResume_Click(sender As Object, e As EventArgs)
42                              Handles btnResume.Click
43          If reader IsNot Nothing Then
44              If reader.State = SynthesizerState.Paused Then
45                  reader.Resume()
46              End If
47          End If
48      End Sub
```

```vb
49    Private Sub btnStop_Click(sender As Object, e As EventArgs)
50                            Handles btnStop.Click
51        If reader IsNot Nothing Then
52            reader.Dispose()
53        End If
54    End Sub
55
56    Private Sub btnExit_Click(sender As Object, e As EventArgs) Handles
57                            btnExit.Click
58        Application.Exit()
59    End Sub
60
61    Private Sub RichTextBox1_MouseDown(sender As Object, e As
62            MouseEventArgs) Handles RichTextBox1.MouseDown
63
64        Dim intAnswer As Integer
65
66        If e.Button = System.Windows.Forms.MouseButtons.Right Then
67            intAnswer = MsgBox("Paste Text From Clipboard", vbYesNo)
68            If intAnswer = MsgBoxResult.Yes Then
69                RichTextBox1.Text = Clipboard.GetText
70            End If
71        End If
72    End Sub
73
74    Private Sub BtnClear_Click(sender As Object, e As EventArgs)
75                            Handles btnClear.Click
76        RichTextBox1.Text = ""
77    End Sub
78    End Class
```

Discussion: Text to Speech Example.

In line 01, Imports System.Speech, we import the Microsoft System.Speech assembly. With the classes in this assembly we can do text-to-speech and also speech recognition. In our case we're going to look at the easier one, text-to-speech.

In line 02, Imports System.Speech.Synthesis, we import the *Speech.Synthesis* class to enable text-to-speech.

In line 04, Dim reader As New SpeechSynthesizer, we create a new speech synthesizer called *reader*.

Lines 06 and 07 show the *Click Event* of the *Speak Button* that was created for us when we double-clicked on the speak button.

Line 08, If RichTextBox1.Text <> "" Then, shows the condition of an if statement. The condition will be true if the rich text box contains any text. We actually test if the text property of the text box is not equal to an empty string. If the condition is true control is passed to the next statement in line nine.

In line 09, reader.Dispose(), we close and clear the *Speech Synthesizer* that we created in line 04, just to get it ready for a new read action.

In line 10, reader = New SpeechSynthesizer, we instantiate a new speech synthesizer called *reader*.

In line 11, reader.SelectVoice(lstboxVoices.Text), we assign the voice from the selected line in the list box called *lstBoxVoices*, to the reader.

In line 12, reader.SpeakAsync(RichTextBox1.Text), we use the *SpeakAsync Method*, of the reader to speak the contents of *RichTextBox1*. We call the async method so that we can do other actions while the reader is reading. If we didn't use async we would have had to wait till the entire contents of the text box was read before we could carry on. This would negate the pause, resume, and stop actions.

Line 13, Else, starts the false part of the condition in line 08. In other words if the text box didn't contain any text.

In line 14, MessageBox.Show("Please enter text"), we use the show method of a *MessageBox Dialogue* to show a message to the user and wait for a response.

You will see that we supplied the message to be displayed as text in the parameter of the show event. Because we didn't specify the buttons to be displayed it used the default which you see here.

Line 15 ends the if statement.

Lines 17 and 18 show the *Click Event* of the *Pause Button* that was created for us when we double-clicked on the pause button.

Line 19, If reader IsNot Nothing Then, we check to see if the *reader* actually exists.

Line 20, If reader.State = SynthesizerState.Speaking Then, which is an if nested in another if, we look at the state of the reader to see if it is actually busy speaking some text. If the condition is true then we can pause the reader as shown in line 21, reader.Pause().

Lines 26 and 27 show the *Load Event* of the *Form* that was created for us when we double-clicked anywhere on the form. This event is automatically called when the form is loaded into memory at the start of execution of the code. Here we can set up anything that must be available at the start of the GUI (Graphical User Interface).

In line 28, Dim lstVoices As New List(Of String)(), we declare a list box called *lstVoices* and instantiate it to an empty list that can contain an array of string values. Remember, in the previous example I said that we can use an index to specify which line to access. Here you have the reason.

In line 29, Dim synth As New SpeechSynthesizer, we declare a *SpeechSynthesizer* called *synth*, and instantiate it to a new speech synthesizer.

In line 31, For Each voice In synth.GetInstalledVoices, we use the *GetInstalledVoices Method* that returns the collection of speech synthesis (text-to-speech) voices that are currently installed on the system. We then iterate through the collection of installed voices by means of the *For Each* loop.

In line 32, lstVoices.Add(voice.VoiceInfo.Name), we use the add method of the list box to add the *Name* properties of each voice in the *VoiceInfo* class to a segment in the list *lstVoices*.

In line 35, For Each child In lstVoices, we use the *For Each* loop to iterate through the list called *lstVoices*.

In line 36, lstboxVoices.Items.Add(child), we add each voice in the voices list to a line in the list box called *lstboxVoices*.

In line 38, lstboxVoices.SetSelected(0, True), we select the first item in the list box called *lstboxVoices*. The zero in the parameter of the *SetSelected* method of the list box places control on the first line in the list box, and the Boolean value *True* selects that specific item.

Lines 41 and 42 show the *Click Event* of the *Resume Button* that was created for us when we double-clicked on the resume button.

Line 43, If reader IsNot Nothing Then, we check to see if the *reader* actually exists.

Line 44, If reader.State = SynthesizerState.Paused Then, which is an if nested in another if, we look at the state of the reader to see if it is paused. If the condition is true then we can Resume the reader as shown in line 45, reader.Resume().

Lines 49 and 50 show the *Click Event* of the *Stop Button* that was created for us when we double-clicked on the stop button.

Line 51, If reader IsNot Nothing Then, we check to see if the *reader* actually exists.

If the reader does exist the statement in line 52, reader.Dispose(), disposes the reader and all of the resources it used.

Lines 56 and 57 show the *Click Event* of the *Exit Button* that was created for us when we double-clicked on the exit button.

In line 58, Application.Exit(), we use the *Exit Method* of the running application to inform all message pumps that they must terminate, and then closes all application windows after the messages have been processed.

Message pumps are said to "pump" messages from the program's *message queue* into the program for processing.

The code in the following two lines (61 and 62) was generated for us. We got to this event by clicking once on the rich text box to get to the properties window. Then we clicked on the lightning bolt as shown in the graphic. We RichTextBox1 System. then looked for the *MouseDown Event*, selected it , and pressed Enter on the keyboard. Enter will take you to the event code as seen in lines 61 and 62.

In line 61, Private Sub RichTextBox1_MouseDown(sender As Object, e As, and 62, MouseEventArgs) Handles RichTextBox1.MouseDown, we capture the *MouseDown* event of the rich text box. The part *Handles RichTextBox1.MouseDown*, specifies which event of the rich text box it handles.

An event handler is a method that is bound to an event. When the event is raised, the code within the event handler is executed. Each event handler provides two parameters that allow you to handle the event properly.

Before we continue, let's clear something up first that will make the event-parameters for the *MouseDown* event clearer.

The *MouseDown Event* is triggered when one of the mouse buttons is clicked. The first parameter, *sender*, provides a reference to the object that raised the event and is specified by, *sender As Object*. The second parameter, *e*, in the example above, passes an object specific to the event that is being handled. By referencing the object's properties, and sometimes its methods, you can obtain information such as the location of the mouse for mouse events, or data being transferred in drag-and-drop events.

The code, *e As MouseEventArgs*, provides data for the *MouseUp, MouseDown,* and *MouseMove* events.

In line 64, Dim intAnswer As Integer, we create an integer variable to contain the value returned from the Message Box we're going to use.

In line 66, If e.Button = System.Windows.Forms.MouseButtons.Right Then, we check against the condition of the if statement to see if it returns true. The

MouseButtons property gets a value indicating which of the mouse buttons is in a pressed state. We're checking to see if the right mouse button was pressed. If it was, then our condition returns *True*, and control is passed to the next line in the code.

In line 67, intAnswer = MsgBox("Paste Text From Clipboard?", vbYesNo), we display a MsgBox with the message "Paste Text From Clipboard?" and the VB constant *vbYesNo*. The message box is a special dialog box used to display a piece of information to the user. The user cannot type anything in the dialog box, but can click on any of the buttons displayed. To support message boxes, **VB** provides a function named *MsgBox*. In our case two buttons are supplied as shown below. We specified it with vbYesNo.

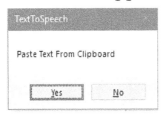

In line 68, If answer = MsgBoxResult.Yes Then, we use an if statement to check if the *Yes* button has been pressed. The result of the message box is an enumeration of the constant returned by the message box. In our case it will be assigned to the variable *intAnswer*. A list of results follows after our discussion.

The code in line 69, RichTextBox1.Text = Clipboard.GetText, is executed if the if statement evaluates to true. In other words the right mouse button has been clicked. Here we use the *GetText* method of the clipboard to retrieve text from the clipboard and assign it to the *Text Method* of the rich text box called *RichTextBox1*.

List of Values for Message Dialogue

Abort	3	**Abort** button was pressed. This member is equivalent to the Visual Basic constant vbAbort.
Cancel	2	**Cancel** button was pressed. This member is equivalent to the Visual Basic constant vbCancel.
Ignore	5	**Ignore** button was pressed. This member is equivalent to the Visual Basic constant vbIgnore.

No	7	**No** button was pressed. This member is equivalent to the Visual Basic constant `vbNo`.
Ok	1	**OK** button was pressed. This member is equivalent to the Visual Basic constant `vbOK`.
Retry	4	**Retry** button was pressed. This member is equivalent to the Visual Basic constant `vbRetry`.
Yes	6	**Yes** button was pressed. This member is equivalent to the Visual Basic constant `vbYes`.

Our last code is in Lines 74 and 75. It shows the *Click Event* of the *Clear Button* that was created for us when we double-clicked on the clear button.

In line 76, RichTextBox1.Text = "", we clear the rich text box by assigning an empty string to the *Text* property.

Unfortunately, for obvious reasons, we don't have any output to show for this program.

CONCLUSION

So, we come to the end of this exercise in programming in Visual Basic. We've only scraped the skim off the top. A book about everything in VB will consist of more than a thousand text-only pages. That was not the idea behind this book. The idea here was just to whet your appetite for more. I hope I have succeeded in that regard.

To discover more, and solve the VB problems you may have, you can visit the site associated with this book at:

https://mailchi.mp/8bbe355fe540/vb-book-code

Happy hunting.

Frans Van Wyk

APPENDIX A

To make it easier to download and install Visual Studio 2019 I include this shortened version of the doc available at Microsoft Docs: https://docs.microsoft.com/en-us/visualstudio/install/install-visual-studio?view=vs-2019

INSTALL VISUAL STUDIO 2019

[NB] This topic applies to Visual Studio on Windows. For Visual Studio for Mac, see **Install Visual Studio for Mac**.

STEP 1 - MAKE SURE YOUR COMPUTER IS READY FOR VISUAL STUDIO

Before you begin installing Visual Studio:

1. Check the system requirements. These requirements help you know whether your computer supports Visual Studio 2019.
2. Apply the latest Windows updates. These updates ensure that your computer has both the latest security updates and the required system components for Visual Studio.
3. Reboot. The reboot ensures that any pending installs or updates don't hinder the Visual Studio install.
4. Free up space. Remove unneeded files and applications from your %SystemDrive% by, for example, running the Disk Cleanup app.

STEP 2 - DOWNLOAD VISUAL STUDIO

Next, download the Visual Studio bootstrapper file. To do so, enter the following link in your browser:

https://visualstudio.microsoft.com/downloads/?utm_medium=microsoft&utm_source=docs.microsoft.com&utm_campaign=button+cta&utm_content=download+vs2019

STEP 3 - INSTALL THE VISUAL STUDIO INSTALLER

Run the bootstrapper file to install the Visual Studio Installer. This new lightweight installer includes everything you need to both install and customize Visual Studio.

1. From your **Downloads** folder, double-click the bootstrapper that matches or is similar to one of the following files:

   - **vs_community.exe** for Visual Studio Community
   - **vs_professional.exe** for Visual Studio Professional
   - **vs_enterprise.exe** for Visual Studio Enterprise

   If you receive a User Account Control notice, choose **Yes**.

2. We'll ask you to acknowledge the Microsoft License Terms and the Microsoft Privacy Statement. Choose **Continue**.

STEP 4 - CHOOSE WORKLOADS

After the installer is installed, you can use it to customize your installation by selecting the feature sets — or workloads — that you want. Here's how.

1. After the new workloads and components are installed, choose **Launch**.

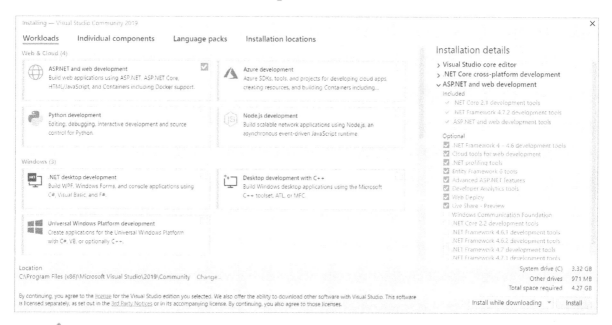

For example, choose the "ASP.NET and web development" workload. It comes with the default core editor, which includes basic code editing support for over 20 languages, the ability to open and edit code from any folder without requiring a project, and integrated source code control.

2. After you choose the workload(s) you want, choose **Install**.

While installing, status screens appear that show the progress of your Visual Studio installation.

At any time after installation, you can install workloads or components that you didn't install initially. If you have Visual Studio open, go to **Tools > Get Tools and Features...** which opens the Visual Studio Installer. Or, open **Visual Studio Installer** from the Start menu. From there, you can choose the workloads or components that you wish to install. Then, choose **Modify**.

STEP 5 - SELECT INDIVIDUAL COMPONENTS (OPTIONAL)

If you don't want to use the Workloads feature to customize your Visual Studio installation, or you want to add more components than a workload installs, you can do so by installing or adding individual components from the **Individual components** tab. Choose what you want, and then follow the prompts.

STEP 6 - INSTALL LANGUAGE PACKS (OPTIONAL)

By default, the installer program tries to match the language of the operating system when it runs for the first time. To install Visual Studio in a language of your choosing, choose the **Language packs** tab from the Visual Studio Installer, and then follow the prompts.

Change the installer language from the command line

Another way that you can change the default language is by running the installer from the command line. For example, you can force the installer to run in English by using the following command: vs_installer.exe --locale en-US. The installer will remember this setting when it is run the next time. The installer supports the following language tokens: zh-cn, zh-tw, cs-cz, en-us, es-es, fr-fr, de-de, it-it, ja-jp, ko-kr, pl-pl, pt-br, ru-ru, and tr-tr.

STEP 7 - CHANGE THE INSTALLATION LOCATION (OPTIONAL)

You can now reduce the installation footprint of Visual Studio on your system drive. You can choose to move the download cache, shared components, SDKs, and tools to different drives, and keep Visual Studio on the drive that runs it the fastest.

Important

You can select a different drive only when you first install Visual Studio. If you've already installed it and want to change drives, you must uninstall Visual Studio and then reinstall it.

STEP 8 - START DEVELOPING

1. After Visual Studio installation is complete, click the **Launch** button to get started developing with Visual Studio.

2. On the start window, choose **Create a new project**.

3. In the search box, enter the type of app you want to create to see a list of available templates. The list of templates depends on the workload(s) that you chose during installation. To see different templates, choose different workloads.

   You can also filter your search for a specific programming language by using the **Language** drop-down list. You can filter by using the **Platform** list and the **Project type** list, too.

4. Visual Studio opens your new project, and you're ready to code!

GLOSSARY

A Program

- A **program** is a set of instructions that a computer follows in order to perform a particular task.

Algorithm

- A procedure or formula for solving a problem, based on conducting a sequence of specified actions.

Alphanumeric Variables

- Variables that store data that are seen as non-numeric. Numeric characters like 0,1 etc. are still handled as text. For programming purposes, alphanumeric data must be shown in quotes.

And Operator

- Performs a logical conjunction on two Boolean expressions, or a bitwise conjunction on two numeric expressions.

AndAlso operator

- Performs short-circuiting logical conjunction on two expressions which means that if the first expression is False, then the second expression is not evaluated.

Append

- Append means to add to the end of.

Application.Cells(1, 1).Value

- Sets the Value property of the specified cell (1,1) of the cells collection in a Worksheet. The numbering of the cells is the same as for a table; the row first then the column.

Application.Exit()

- Informs all message pumps that they must terminate, and then closes all application windows after the messages have been processed.

Arithmetic Operators

- Perform familiar calculations on numeric values, including shifting their bit patterns.

Array Index

- A number used to identify an individual element based on its position in the array. The indexes of an array range from 0 to one less than the total number of elements in the array.

Array.Reverse()

- An Array object inherits from the System.Array class, and the Reverse method of the Array Class reverses the elements in the array.

Array.Sort()

- An Array object inherits from the System.Array class, and the sort method of the Array Class sorts the elements in the array in ascEnding order.

Arrays

- An array is a set of values, which are termed elements, that are logically related to each other. By using an array, you can refer to these related values by the same name, and use a number that's called an index or subscript to identify an individual element based on its position in the array.

As Clause

- Identifies a data type in a declaration statement or a constraint list on a generic type parameter.

ASCII

- **ASCII** (American Standard Code for Information Interchange) is the most common format for text files in computers and on the Internet. In an **ASCII** file, each alphabetic, numeric, or special character is represented with a 7-bit binary number (a string of seven 0s or 1s). 128 possible characters are defined.

Assignment Operators

- Are used to assign a value to the operand to the left of the operator.

Asynchronously

- Controlling the timing of operations by the use of pulses sent when the previous operation is completed rather than at regular intervals, which allows the CPU to continue processing with other data that is independent of the current I/O operation.

Base Class

- A base class is a class, in an object-oriented programming language, from which other classes are derived. It facilitates the creation of other classes that can reuse the code implicitly inherited from the base class.

Binary System

- A system in which information can only be expressed by combinations of the digits 0 and 1.

Bit

- A bit (short for "binary digit") is the smallest unit of measurement used to quantify computer data. It contains a single binary value of 0 or 1.

Boolean

- Holds values that can be only True or False. The keywords True and False correspond to the two states of Boolean variables.

Bubble sort

- Bubble sort is a sorting algorithm that works by repeatedly swapping adjacent elements if they are in wrong order.

Button Control
- Presents a standard button that the user can click to perform actions.

ByRef
- Specifies that an argument is passed in such a way that the called procedure can change the value of a variable underlying the argument in the calling code.

Byte
- The byte is a unit of digital information that most commonly consists of eight bits, representing a binary number. It is usually the smallest addressable unit of memory in a computer.

ByVal
- Specifies that an argument is passed in such a way that the called procedure or property cannot change the value of a variable underlying the argument in the calling code.

Camel Casing
- The camelCasing convention, used for naming variables, fields and parameters, capitalizes the first character of each word except the first word.

Case insensitive
- That means that an uppercase letter is not distinct from a lowercase letter. The VB language is case insensitive, but things like string searches are not.

Cdec
- Cdec is an internal Function in Visual Basic and is used to convert a string expression into a decimal datatype. This function uses the local settings of your system for conversion.

Central Processing Unit (CPU)
- This is the electronic circuitry within a computer that carries out the instructions of a computer program by performing the basic arithmetic, logic, controlling, and input/output (I/O) operations specified by the instructions.

Char.ToUpper Method
- Converts the value of an ASCII or Unicode character to its uppercase equivalent.

CheckBox Control
- Indicates whether a condition is on or off.

CheckedListBox Control
- Displays a list of items with a check box next to each item.

Class
- In object-oriented programming, a class is an extensible program-code-template for creating objects, providing initial values for state (member variables) and implementations of behavior (member functions or methods).

Class Statement

- A Class statement defines a new data type, declares the name of a class and introduces the definition of the variables, properties, events, and procedures that the class comprises.

Click Event

- Occurs when the control is clicked.

Clipboard.GetText Method

- Retrieves text data from the Clipboard.

Close()

- When used with a streamwriter or streamreader it closes the appropriate textreader or -writer.

cmd /C

- The command prompt (Dos prompt) *cmd* starts a new instance of the Windows command interpreter. In this case it is called with the /C switch. This switch carries out the command specified by the string following it, and then terminates.

Columns.AutoFit()

- Sets the AutoFit property of all the columns in the worksheet, with the result that the columns fit the contents of each cell in that specific column.

ComboBox Control

- Displays data in a drop-down combo box.

Comments

- Comments are brief explanatory notes added to code for the benefit of those reading it, and is preceded on the same line by the comment symbol ' (single quotation mark).

Comparison Operators

- Compare two expressions and return a Boolean value representing the result of the comparison.

Compiler

- a program that converts instructions into a machine-code or lower-level form so that they can be read and executed by a computer.

Compiling

- To convert (a program) into a machine-code or lower-level form in which the program can be executed.

Computer

- An electronic device for storing and processing data according to instructions given to it in a variable program.

Concatenation Operators

- Join multiple strings into a single string.

Console

- A console is an operating system window through which a user can communicate with the operating system, or we can say a console is an application in which we can give text as an input from the keyboard and get the text as an output from the computer.

Console Application

- A console application is a computer program designed to be used via a text-only computer interface, such as a text terminal, or a command line interface of some operating systems (Unix, DOS, etc.). A user typically interacts with a console application using only a keyboard and display screen.

Console Class

- Represents the standard input, output, and error streams for console applications. This class cannot be inherited.

Console.BackgroundColor Property

- Gets or sets the background color of the console. A value that specifies the background color of the console; that is, the color that appears behind each character. The default is black.

Console.Clear() Method

- Clears the console buffer and corresponding console window of display information.

Console.ForegroundColor Property

- Gets or sets the foreground color of the console. A value that specifies the foreground color of the console; that is, the color of each character that is displayed. The default is gray.

Console.Read()

- Reads the next character from the standard input stream.

Console.ReadKey() Method

- Obtains the next character or function key pressed by the user. The pressed key is displayed in the console window.

Console.ReadLine()

- Reads the next line of characters from the standard input stream. If the standard input device is the keyboard, the readline method blocks execution until the user presses the Enter key.

Console.Title Property

- Gets or sets the title to display in the console title bar. The string to be displayed in the title bar of the console. The maximum length of the title string is 24500 characters.

Console.Write Method
- Writes the text representation of the specified value or values to the standard output stream without the current line terminator.

Console.WriteLine() Method
- A Method of the Console Class that writes the specified data, followed by the current line terminator, to the standard output stream.

Const
- Declares and defines one or more constants.

Constants
- A constant is a value that cannot be altered by the program during normal execution

Constructor
- A constructor is a special type of subroutine called to create an object. It prepares the new object for use, often accepting arguments that the constructor uses to set required member variables. A constructor resembles an instance method, but it differs from a method in that it has no explicit return type, it is not implicitly inherited, and it usually has different rules for scope modifiers.

Continue Do Statement
- This transfers control to the next iteration of the *Do loop*.

Continue For
- Transfers control to the next loop iteration before the Next statement is reached.

Control
- A control is an individually distinct user interface (UI) element that displays data or accepts data input.

Control Structures
- Control structures allow you to regulate the flow of your program's execution.

Convert Class
- Converts a base data type to another base data type.

Counter (in a For Loop)
- **Counter** is required in the *For* statement. Counter is a *Numeric* variable and is the control variable for the loop.

CreateObject("wscript.shell")
- Instantiate an instance of an outside application into the VBscript runtime. Basically, in the case of wscript.shell, it creates an object that is an instance of the Windows **shell**, allowing you to run commands against the Windows shell from within your VBScript.

CreateObject() Method

- Creates and returns a reference to a COM object. CreateObject cannot be used to create instances of classes in Visual Basic, unless those classes are explicitly exposed as COM components.

Data

- The quantities, characters, or symbols on which operations are performed by a computer. It can be something simple and seemingly random and useless until it is organized.

Data Type

- A particular kind of data item, as defined by the values it can take, the programming language used, or the operations that can be performed on it.

DateTimePicker Control

- Allows the user to select a single item from a list of dates or times.

Decimal Data Type

- The Decimal data type provides the greatest number of significant digits for a number. It supports up to 29 significant digits and can represent values in excess of 7.9228×10^{28}. It is particularly suitable for calculations, such as financial, that require a large number of digits but cannot tolerate rounding errors.

Dim Statement

- Declares and allocates storage space for one or more variables.

Dispose Method (SpeechSynthesizer)

- Disposes the SpeechSynthesizer object and releases resources used during the session.

Do Statement

- Starts the definition of the Do loop

Do...Loop

- Repeats a set of statements an indefinite number of times, until a condition is satisfied.

Do...While...Loop Statement

- Repeats a block of statements while a Boolean condition is True

Documents.Add method (Word)

- Returns a Document object that represents a new, empty document added to the collection of open documents.

Documents.Open method (Word)

- Opens the specified document and adds it to the Documents collection. Returns a Document object.

Double

- The Double data type provides the largest and smallest possible magnitudes for a number. It holds signed IEEE 64-bit (8-byte) double-precision floating-point numbers that range in value from -1.79769313486231570E+308 through -4.94065645841246544E-324 for negative values and from 4.94065645841246544E-324 through 1.79769313486231570E+308 for positive values.

e parameter
- By convention, "e" is the variable used to define any arguments for the event. Depending on the event, e can have any number of properties and methods.

e.Button
- Gets which mouse button was pressed.

Else
- The part of the If …Then…Else selection statement that defines the code that will be executed if the condition returns False.

Encapsulation
- The action of enclosing something in, or as if in a capsule.In programming terms the same as information hiding.

End Class Statement
- Terminates the Class definition.

End Function statement
- Ends the function and returns control to the calling statement.

End If
- Ends the If …Then…Else selection statement.

End Module Statement
- Terminates the Module definition.

End Select Statement
- Terminates the definition of the Select…Case construction.

End Statement
- Terminates execution immediately.

End Structure Statement
- Closes the structure declared by the Structure Statement.

End Using
- Terminates the definition of the Using block and disposes of all the resources that it controls.

Environment Class
- Retrieves information about directories and logical drives.

Environment.CurrentDirectory Property
- Gets or sets the fully qualified path of the current working directory.

Event
- An event is an action recognized by an object, such as clicking the mouse or pressing a key, and for which you can write code to respond.

EventArgs Class
- Represents the base class for classes that contain event data, and provides a value to use for events that do not include event data.

Exit Do Statement
- This transfers control out of the Do loop.

Exit For
- Transfers control out of the For loop.

External memory
- Stores data outside of the CPU and internal memory. It can be in the form of some sort of storing device like a hard disk, or a USB memory stick etc.

Field
- Fields are the individual parts that contain information about the record.

File
- A file can be seen as a collection of records about something like, for instance, employees.

File.Exists(String) Method
- The string represents the path and this method merely checks if the file specified in the path exists.

FileAccess
- The fileAccess argument is a member of the FileAccess enumeration and specifies what type of access is allowed for the operating system to handle a file.

FileAccess.Read
- Sets the access to a specific file to read.

FileAccess.Write
- Sets the access to a specific file to write.

FileMode
- The fileMode argument is a member of the FileMode enumeration and specifies how the operating system should open a file.

FileMode.Open Method
- Opens a FileStream on the specified path.

Flowchart
- A flowchart is a type of diagram that represents an algorithm, workflow or process. Flowchart can also be defined as a diagramatic representation of an algorithm (step by step approach to solve a task).

Flush() Method
- Clears buffers for a FileStream stream and causes any buffered data to be written to the file.

Font.Color Property

- Returns or sets the font color in the specified range. VB constants cannot be used, only integer values.

Font.Size property (Word)

- Returns or sets the font size, in points. Read/write **Single**.

For Each Loop

- Runs a set of statements once for each element in a collection.

For Each...Next

- The For Each...Next construction runs a set of statements once for each element in a collection. You specify the loop control variable, but you do not have to determine starting or ending values for it.

For Loop

- Performs the loop a set number of times.

For...Next

- The For...Next construction performs the loop a set number of times. It uses a loop control variable, also called a counter, to keep track of the repetitions. You specify the starting and ending values for this counter, and you can optionally specify the amount by which it increases from one repetition to the next.

Form

- A form is a visual interface on which you display information to the user.

Format() Method

- Returns a string formatted according to instructions contained in a format String expression.

Format.SpaceAfter property (Word)

- Returns or sets the amount of spacing (in points) after the specified paragraph or text column. Read/write Single.

Forms Applications

- Windows Forms (WinForms) is a graphical (GUI) class library included as a part of Microsoft .NET Framework or Mono Framework, providing a platform to write rich client applications for desktop, laptop, and tablet PCs. A Windows Forms application is built on classes from the Windows.Forms namespace that forms part of the System Namespace.

Function Statement

- Declares the name, parameters, and code that define a Function procedure. A **Function** procedure is a series of **Visual Basic** statements enclosed by the **Function** and **End Function** statements. The **Function** procedure performs a task and then returns control to the calling code. When it returns control, it also returns a value to the calling code.

GetInstalledVoices Method (SpeechSynthesizer)
- Returns the collection of speech synthesis (text-to-speech) voices that are currently installed on the system.

Handles Clause
- Declares that a procedure handles a specified event.

High-level programming language
- Any programming language that enables development of a program in a much more user-friendly programming context, and is generally independent of the computer's hardware architecture. It is more like human language and less like machine language.

IDE
- An **IDE** (Integrated Development Environment) normally consists of at least a source code editor, build automation tools, and a debugger.

Identifiers
- **Identifiers** are names that programmers choose for a class, variable, function, or any other user-defined item. An **identifier** must begin with a letter.

If
- Starts the If …Then…Else selection statement.

If...Then...Else
- Conditionally executes a group of statements, depending on the value of an expression.

Imports Statement
- Imports namespaces from a specified assembly.

Information
- Data that is processed, organized, structured or presented in a specific context so as to make it useful.

Information hiding
- Information hiding as a way in which clients (users as well as program components) can be shielded from the internal working of a program.

Inheritance
- Is the process of creating a new Class, called the Derived Class, from the existing class, called the Base Class. Inheritance is a very elegant way to reuse and modify the data and functionality that has already been defined in the Base Class. New data and functionality can be added to the Derived Class. Since the Derived Class inherits all properties of the Base Class, the Derived Class has a larger set of properties than the Base Class. However, the Derived Class may override some or all the properties of the Base Class.

Instance
- An instance is a specific object created from a particular class.

Instantiate

- The act of creating an instance of a Class is called instantiation. To instantiate a class is to create an object of that class. Each instantiation is unique, depending on the different elements and values in that object.

Integer

- A number which is not a fraction; a whole number. An Integer data type holds signed 32-bit (4-byte) integers that range in value from -2,147,483,648 through 2,147,483,647.

Integrated Development Environment

- An integrated development environment (IDE) is a software application that provides comprehensive facilities to computer programmers for software development.

Internal Memory

- All of the storage spaces that are accessible by a processor without the use of the computer input-output channels. It is usually connected directly to the motherboard.

Interpreter

- An **interpreter** is a computer program that can analyse and execute instructions written in a programming or scripting language. It does this line by line, without requiring them previously to have been compiled into a machine language program.

IsNot Operator

- The IsNot operator determines if two object references refer to different objects. However, it does not perform value comparisons. If object1 and object2 both refer to the exact same object instance, result is False; if they do not, result is True.

Items.Add Method

- Adds an item to the list of items for a ListBox.

Iteration

- Visual Basic Iteration (loop) structures allow you to run one or more lines of code repetitively. You can repeat the statements in a loop structure until a condition is True, until a condition is False, a specified number of times, or once for each element in a collection.

Label Control

- Displays text that cannot be edited by the user.

LinkLabel Control

- Allows you to add Web-style links to Windows Forms applications.

List()
- It represents an ordered collection of an object that can be indexed individually. It is basically an alternative to an array. However, unlike array, you can add and remove items from a list at a specified position using an index, and the array resizes itself automatically.

ListBox Control
- Allows the user to select one or more items from a predefined list.

ListBox.Items Property
- Gets the items of the ListBox.

ListView Control
- Displays a list of items with icons, in the manner of Windows Explorer.

Logical Operators
- Evaluate one or more expressions and return a Boolean value depending on the outcome.

Long
- A **long** integer is a number that can be used for a variable involving greater numbers than integers. It holds signed 64-bit (8-byte) integers ranging in value from -9,223,372,036,854,775,808 through 9,223,372,036,854,775,807 (9.2...E+18).

Loop Statement
- Terminates the definition of the Do loop.

Machine code
- Machine code, also known as machine language, is the elemental language of computers. It can be read by the computer's central processing unit (CPU), and is composed of digital binary numbers. It looks like a very long sequence of zeros and ones, and can be directly executed by the computer without any conversion or translation.

MaskedTextBox Control
- Constrains the format of user input in a form.

Me
- The Me keyword provides a way to refer to the specific instance of a class or structure in which the code is currently executing. Me behaves like either an object variable or a structure variable referring to the current instance. Using Me is particularly useful for passing information about the currently executing instance of a class or structure to a procedure in another class, structure, or module.

MessageBox Class
- Controls the display of a message window, also known as a dialog box, which presents a message to the user. It is a modal window, blocking other actions in the application until the user closes it. A MessageBox can contain text, buttons, and symbols that inform and instruct the user.

MessageBox.Show Method
- Displays a message box.

Method
- A method is an action that an object can perform.

Microsoft Visual Studio
- Microsoft Visual Studio is an integrated development environment (IDE) from Microsoft. It is used to develop computer programs, as well as websites, web apps, web services and mobile apps.

Module
- Every module has exactly one instance and does not need to be created or assigned to a variable. Modules do not support inheritance or implement interfaces. It provides a way to declare variables that live outside of any single routine and don't go away when you exit the routine, and an easy way to associate which code/module(s) are in which source files.

Module Statement
- Declares the name of a module and introduces the definition of the variables, properties, events, and procedures that the module comprises. A Module statement defines a reference type available throughout its namespace.

Monospaced font
- A font whose letters and characters each occupy the same amount of horizontal space. Also called a non-proportional font.

MonthCalendar Control
- Presents an intuitive graphical interface for users to view and set date information.

MouseButtons.Right
- The right mouse button was pressed.

MouseDown
- Occurs when the mouse pointer is over the control and a mouse button is pressed.

MouseEventArgs
- Provides data for the MouseUp, MouseDown, and MouseMove events.

MsgBox function
- Displays a message in a dialog box, waits for the user to click a button, and returns an Integer indicating which button the user clicked.

MsgBoxResult.Yes
- Yes button was pressed. This member is equivalent to the Visual Basic constant vbYes.

MyBase
- The MyBase keyword behaves like an object variable referring to the base class of the current instance of a class.

MyBase.Load
- Loads the base class of the current instance of a class.

Name property
- The Name property is a string used by clients to identify, find, or announce an object for the user. All objects support the Name property.

Namespace Statement
- A **namespace** is a declarative region that provides a scope to the identifiers (the names of types, functions, variables, etc.) inside it. **Namespaces are** used to organize code into logical groups and to prevent name collisions that **can** occur especially when your code base includes multiple libraries.

New
- The New clause is used to create a new object instance, specifies a constructor constraint on a type parameter, or identifies a Sub procedure as a class constructor. A New clause can be used in a declaration statement or an assignment statement. When the statement runs, it calls the appropriate constructor of the specified class, passing any supplied arguments.

Next
- Terminates the definition of the For loop.

Non-primitive data types
- Non-primitive data types are not defined by the programming language, but are instead created by the programmer. They are sometimes called "reference variables," or "object references," since they reference a memory location, which stores the data.

Nothing
- Represents the default value of any data type. For reference types, the default value is the null reference. For value types, the default value depends on whether the value type is nullable. VB uses the keyword **Nothing** for **null** values.

NotifyIcon Component
- Displays icons for processes that run in the background and would not otherwise have user interfaces.

Numeric Variables
- Variables for handling numbers in various representations. Integral types represent only whole numbers (positive, negative, and zero), and nonintegral types represent numbers with both integer and fractional parts.

NumericUpDown Control
- Displays numerals that a user can browse through and select from.

Object
- **Object** refers to a particular instance of a class, where the **object** can be a combination of variables, functions, and data structures.

Object-Oriented Language
- An Object-oriented language is a programming language model in which programs are organized around objects, which can contain data, in the form of fields (often known as *attributes)*, and code, in the form of procedures (often known as *methods)* rather than functions and logic.

Of Clause
- Identifies a type parameter on a generic class, structure, interface, delegate, or procedure.

OpenTextFileReader() Method
- Opens a StreamReader object to read from the file specified in the brackets. It is a method of the Computer.FileSystem Class.

OpenTextFileWriter() Method
- Opens a StreamWriter object to write to the file specified in the brackets. It is a method of the Computer.FileSystem Class.

Operating System
- The low-level software that supports a computer's basic functions, such as scheduling tasks and controlling peripherals.

Operand
- The values the operator acts upon are called *operands.*

Operator
- An *operator* is a code element that performs an operation on one or more code elements that hold values.

Operator Precedence
- The predetermined order in which each part is evaluated and resolved when several operations occur in an expression.

Paragraphs.Add method (Word)
- Returns a Paragraph object that represents a new, blank paragraph added to a document.

Parameters
- Parameters are used by procedures and functions to pass information in and out. They are used in the definition and in the call of these constructs. The parameters used in the procedure/function definition are called the formal parameters. The parameters used in the procedure/function **call** are called the actual parameters.

Pascal Casing

- The PascalCasing convention, used for classes and structures, enumerations, properties, and methods, capitalizes the first character of each word (including acronyms over two letters in length).

Path.Combine Method

- Combines strings into a path. The path can be either absolute or relative. An absolute path starts at the root directory like c:\abc\def\, while the relative path starts with the directory in relation to the current position.

Pause Method (SpeechSynthesizer)

- Pauses the SpeechSynthesizer object.

PictureBox Control

- Displays graphics in bitmap, GIF, JPEG, metafile, or icon format.

Polymorphism

- Polymorphism is the ability of an object to behave differently under different conditions.

Presentations.Open method (PowerPoint)

- Opens the specified presentation. Returns a Presentation object that represents the opened presentation.

Preserve

- Optional statement used with the ReDim Statement. It is a modifier used to preserve the data in the existing array when you change the size of only the last dimension.

Primitive data types

- An elementary data structure that is supported natively by a programming language and cannot be decomposed into simpler components.

Private

- The Private keyword in the declaration statement specifies that the element can be accessed only from within the same module, class, or structure.

Procedure

- A Procedure is also known as a method, a routine, a subroutine, or a function, and contains a collection of code that belongs and works together to accomplish one outcome.

Programming language

- A programming language is a set of commands, instructions, and other syntax used to create a software program through the use of syntactic and semantic rules, to determine structure and meaning respectively.

ProgressBar Control

- Graphically indicates the progress of an action towards completion.

Project

- In Visual Studio, you start with a project. In a logical sense, a project contains all the source code files, icons, images, data files, etc. that are compiled into an executable, library, or website. A project also contains compiler settings and other configuration files that might be needed by various services or components that your program communicates with.

Properties

- Properties are the attributes that describe something.

Public statement.

- Specifies that one or more declared programming elements have no access restrictions.

RadioButton Control

- Presents a set of two or more mutually exclusive options to the user.

Range.Font property (Word)

- Returns or sets a Font object that represents the character formatting of the specified object. Read/write Font.

Range.Font.Bold Property (Word)

- Returns or sets the bold property for the font. True if the font is bold. False if it is not bold. Read/write Variant.

Range.InsertParagraphAfter method (Word)

- Inserts a paragraph mark after a range. After this method is applied, the range expands to include the new paragraph.

Range.Text property (Word)

- Returns or sets the text in the specified range or selection. Read/write String.

Readkey().KeyChar

- Uses the KeyChar property of the Readkey() method to report the key that was pressed. It returns a character type (Char).

ReadToEnd()

- It is a method of the StreamReader Class and reads all characters from the current position to the end of the stream.

Real Numbers

- A real number is a number that can be positive or negative and have decimal places after the point.

Record

- A record is a group of fields that are relevant to a specific entity.

ReDim

- You can use the ReDim statement to change the size of one or more dimensions of an array that has already been declared. It will clear all values already stored in the array.

Return Statement
- The Return statement simultaneously assigns the return value and exits a function. Follow the return keyword with an expression that yields the value you want to return to the calling code

Return values
- The "return value" is the value a Function procedure sends back to the calling code. Usually the value at the right hand side of an assignment.

RichTextBox Control
- Allows users to enter, display, and manipulate text with formatting.

Run Command (for WshShell)
- We use Run when we are calling an external command-line program (or any command that the prompt recognizes).

Scope
- The *scope* of a declared element is the set of all code that can refer to it without qualifying its name or making it available through an Imports statement.

Scripting language
- A scripting language is a programming language designed for integrating and communicating with other programming languages.

Select Case Statement
- Runs one of several groups of statements, depending on the value of an expression.

Selection
- Controlling the flow of logic in a program by means of the If or Select statements.

SelectVoice Method
- A method of the Speechsynthesizer class that selects a specific voice by name.

Semantics
- The meaning of linguistic expressions.

Sender parameter.
- By convention, "sender" is the variable used to define which object generated the event.

Sentinel value
- A sentinel value is a special value that is used to terminate a loop. The sentinel value is typically chosen so as to not be a legitimate data value that the loop will encounter and attempt to perform with.

Sequence
- In a sequence structure, an action, or event, leads to the next ordered action in a predetermined order. The sequence can contain any number of actions, but no actions can be skipped in the sequence.

Sequential file
- A sequential file contains records organized by the order in which they were entered. The order of the records is fixed.

SetSelected Method
- Selects or clears the selection for the specified item in a ListBox.

Shared Statement
- Specifies that one or more declared programming elements are associated with a class or structure at large, and not with a specific instance of the class or structure. Sharing a member of a class or structure makes it available to every instance.

SlideMaster.CustomLayouts
- Represents a set of custom layouts associated with a presentation design. Use the CustomLayouts property of the slide Master object to return a CustomLayouts collection. Use CustomLayouts (index), where index is the custom layout index number, to return a single CustomLayout object.

Slides.AddSlide
- Creates a new slide, adds it to the Slides collection, and returns the slide.

Slides.count
- Returns the number of objects in the specified collection. Read-only.

Solution
- A project is contained within a solution. Despite its name, a solution is not an "answer". It is simply a container for one or more related projects, along with build information, Visual Studio window settings, and any miscellaneous files that aren't associated with a particular project.

Solution Explorer
- The Solution Explorer is a special window that enables you to manage solutions, projects, and files. It provides a complete view of the files in a project, and it enables you to add or remove files and to organize files into subfolders.

SpeakAsync
- A method of the Speechsynthesizer class that Generates speech output asynchronously from a string, a Prompt object, or a PromptBuilder object. The async method is used so that we can do other actions while the reader is reading.

Speaking (SpeechSynthesizer)
- Indicates that the SpeechSynthesizer is currently speaking.

SpeechSynthesizer Class
- Provides access to the functionality of an installed speech synthesis engine.

Split Method (String)

- Allows you to **split** a line of text and put each element (word or phrase) into an array. It returns a string array that contains the substrings that are delimited by elements of a specified string or Unicode character array.

State Property (SpeechSynthesizer)

- Gets the current speaking state of the SpeechSynthesizer object.

Step

- It is the amount by which the counter is incremented each time through the loop. If the optional *Step* statement is not supplied, a step of one is inferred.

StreamReader Class

- The StreamReader class is used to read text from a stream. Implements a TextReader that can read a sequential series of characters from a stream.

StreamWriter Class

- The StreamWriter class is used to write text to a stream. It Implements a TextWriter that can write a sequential series of characters to a stream in a particular encoding.

String

- A linear sequence of characters, words, or other data. The string data type is comprised of a set of characters that can also contain spaces and numbers. A string can contain from 0 to approximately two billion Unicode characters. The value of a string type must be between quotes.

Structure Statement

- Declares the name of a structure and introduces the definition of the variables, properties, events, and procedures that the structure comprises.

Structures

- A *structure* is a generalization of the user-defined type. In addition to fields, structures can expose properties, methods, and events. A structure can implement one or more interfaces, and individual access levels for each field can be declared. Data items of different types can be combined to create a structure. A structure associates one or more *elements* with each other and with the structure itself. When a structure is declared, it becomes a *composite data type*, and variables of that type can be declared.

Sub Statement

- Declares the name, parameters, and code that define a Sub procedure.

Sub Procedure

- A Sub procedure is a series of Visual Basic statements enclosed by the Sub and End Sub statements. The Sub procedure performs a task and then returns control to the calling code, but it does not return a value to the calling code.

Subscript
- The same as an array index.

Syntax
- The set of rules, principles, and processes that govern the structure of sentences in a given language.

System.IO Namespace
- The System.IO namespace contains types that allow reading and writing to files and data streams, and types that provide basic file and directory support.

Text property
- Gets or sets the text associated with a control.

Text To Speech
- Text to speech, is a form of speech synthesis that converts text into spoken voice output.

TextBox Control
- Allows editable, multiline input from the user.

Then
- The part of the If …Then…Else selection statement that defines the code that will be executed if the condition returns True.

To Keyword
- The To keyword is used in the For statement to specify the range for the counter. It can also be used in the Select...Case Statement and in array declarations.

ToDouble Method
- A method of the Convert class that converts the value of a specified object to a double-precision floating-point number.

ToInt16 Method
- A method of the Convert class that converts the value of a specified object to a 16-bit signed integer.

ToInt32 Method
- Converts a specified value to a 32-bit signed integer.

ToolTip Component
- Displays text when the user points at other controls.

ToString() Method
- It converts an object to its string representation so that it is suitable for display. A standard format string contains a single format specifier in the brackets, which is an alphabetic character that defines the string representation of the object to which it is applied, along with an optional precision specifier that affects how many digits are displayed in the result string.

TreeView Control
- Displays a hierarchy of nodes that can be expanded or collapsed, as seen in Windows Explorer.

Ubound Function
- Returns a Long data type containing the largest available subscript for the indicated dimension of an array.

Unicode
- An international encoding standard for use with different languages and scripts, by which each letter, digit, or symbol is assigned a unique numeric value that applies across different platforms and programs. **Unicode** uses a variable bit encoding program where you can choose **between** 32, 16, and 8-bit encodings.

Until Statement
- Repeats the loop until the condition is True.

Using
- Declares the beginning of a Using block and optionally acquires the system resources that the block controls.

Val Method
- Returns the numbers contained in a string as a numeric value of appropriate type.

Variables
- A variable is a reference to a certain cell, or grouping of cells in memory. Data items that may take on more than one value during the runtime of a program.

Variable-width font
- A font where the letters and spacings have different widths to let it look neater when reading.

Variant Data type
- A Variant is a special data type that can contain any kind of data except fixed-length String data.

vbAbort
- Abort button was pressed.

vbBack
- = chr(8) - Backspace character

vbCancel
- Cancel button was pressed.

vbCr
- = chr(13) - Carriage return character

vbCrLf
- = "\n" - Carriage return linefeed combination

vbFormFeed
- = chr(12) - Not useful in Microsoft Windows

vbIgnore
- Ignore button was pressed.

vbLf

- = chr(10) - Linefeed character

vbNewLine
- = "\n" - Platform-specific new line character; whichever is appropriate for the current platform

vbNo
- No button was pressed.

vbNullChar
- = chr(0) - Character having value 0

vbNullString
- = chr(0) - String having value 0. Not the same as a zero-length string (""); used for calling external procedures

vbObjectError
- = -2147221504 - User-defined error umbers should be greater than this value. For example: Err.Raise Number = vbObjectError + 1000

vbOK
- **OK** button was pressed.

vbRetry
- Retry button was pressed.

VBScript
- **VBScript** ("Microsoft Visual Basic Scripting Edition") is an Active Scripting language developed by Microsoft that is modeled on Visual Basic.

vbTab
- = chr(9) - Tab character

vbVerticalTab
- = chr(11) - Not useful in Microsoft Windows

vbYes
- Yes button was pressed.

Visible property (Word)
- Returns, or sets the visibility of the object. True if the specified object is visible, False if it not visible. Read/write Boolean.

Visual Basic .NET
- **Visual Basic .NET (VB.NET)** is a multi-paradigm, object-oriented programming language, implemented on the **.NET** Framework. Microsoft launched **VB.NET** in 2002 as the successor to its original **Visual Basic** language.

WebBrowser Control

- Hosts Web pages and provides Internet Web browsing capabilities to your application.

While Statement

- Repeat a loop until the condition is False.

Windows Shell

- An add-on user interface for Windows. The Windows shell also implements a shell namespace that enables computer programs running on Windows to access the computer's resources via the hierarchy of shell objects.

Workbooks.Add(Object) Method

- Creates a new workbook. The new workbook becomes the active workbook. Returns a Microsoft Excel Workbook object.

Worksheet object (Excel)

- The Worksheet object is a member of the Worksheets collection. The Worksheets collection contains all the Worksheet objects in a workbook. The Worksheet object is also a member of the Sheets collection. The Sheets collection contains all the sheets in the workbook (both chart sheets and worksheets).

WriteLine()

- Writes data to a sequential file when used with a streamwriter. The output is included in the brackets.

WshShell

- WshShell is a generic name for a powerful object that enables you to query and interact with various aspects of the Windows shell. You can display information to the user, run applications, create shortcuts, work with the Registry, and control Windows' environment variables.

INDEX

A

A Program 9,15,22,197
Algorithm 15,16,95,197,198,205
Alphanumeric Variables 26,27,197
And operator 148,150,197
AndAlso operator 148,197
Append 69,72,125,126,136,197
Application.Cells(1, 1).Value 155,197
Application.Exit() 184,197
Arithmetic Operators 197
Array Index 80,197,217
Array.Reverse() 91,197
Array.Sort() 88,91,198
Arrays 79,80,84,85,87,88,91,94,98,99,198
As Clause 198
ASCII 13,198
Assignment Operators 77,198
Asynchronously 198

B

Base Class 31,105,124,194,205,207,210
Binary system 12,13,198
Bit 12,13,76,197,198,199
Boolean 19,29,53,54,61,71,75,77,148,184,
            197,198,200,203,209,220
Bubble sort 95,96,98,99,198
Button Control 162,199
ByRef 94,199
Byte 19,199
ByVal 199

C

Camel Casing 101,111,199
Case insensitive 101,199
Cdec 46,199
Central Processing Unit (CPU) 22,199,209
Char.ToUpper Method 136,199

CheckBox Control 162,199
CheckedListBox Control 162,199
Class 6,19,31,32,34-47,56,71,72,84,88,101,
        107,108,114,118,119,124,125,126,
        129,137,139,149,151,152,170,171,
        172,175,177,182,184,197,198,199,
        211
Class Statement 200
Click Event 173,182,183,184,187,200
Clipboard.GetText Method 186,200
Close() 71,72,119,136,200
cmd /C 139,200
Columns.AutoFit() 155,200
ComboBox Control 162,200
Comments 18,41,84,85,101,200
Comparison Operators 74,147,200
Compiler 12,13,18,46,70,101,200,213
Compiling 13,200
Computer 1,2,9,12,13,15,16,19,22,71,95,
            119,200
Concatenation 76,115,200
Console 80,85,94,102,103,105,106,109,201
Console Application 102,201
Console Class 42,114,201,202
Console.BackgroundColor 201
Console.Clear() 94,201
Console.ForegroundColor 201
Console.Read() 201
Console.ReadKey() 42,94,136,150,201
Console.ReadLine() 56,95,111,126,201
Console.Title 201
Console.Write 36,64,84,114,126,202
Console.WriteLine()35,36,41,46,72,84,
                108,111,128,129,136,202
Const 24,125,135,202
Constants 22,24,73,125,129,135,186,187,
        202
Constructor 34,35,38,202,211
Continue Do Statement 60,61,202

Continue For 62,202

Control 61,62,64,114,120,152,161,167,168, 172,184,186,202

Control Structures 49,202

Convert Class 56,202

Counter (in a For Loop) 62,64,65,202,206, 216,218

CreateObject("wscript.shell")137,139,141, 202

CreateObject() Method 137,139,141,151, 155,203

D

Data 5,6,7,19,22,23,25,26,37,38,67,68,69, 95,107,116,127,139,161,167,173, 177 185,203

Data Type 19,23,28,29,53,54,62,84,107, 139,203

DateTimePicker Control 162,203

Decimal 19,25,46,47,48,203

Dim Statement 23,34,85,203

Dispose Method (SpeechSynthesizer) 182, 184,203

Do Statement 60,203

Do…Loop 203

Do…While…Loop Statement 203

Documents.Add method (Word) 153,203

Documents.Open method (Word) 152, 203

Double 19,46,152,203-204

E

e parameter 204

e.Button 185,204

Else 53,54,149,150,182,204

Encapsulation 5,204

End Class Statement 108,125,204

End Function 115,204,206

End If 53,54,65,137,150,204

End Module Statement 204

End Select Statement 149,204

End Statement 101,108,173,204

End Structure Statement 29,204

End Using 72,120,127,204

Environment Class 151,152,204

Environment.CurrentDirectory 151,204

Event 162,172,185,204

EventArgs Class 172,177,205

Exit Do Statement 205

Exit For 62,205

External memory 22,205

F

Field 67,68,205

File 6,67-72,116-129,131,135,136,137,139,
    151,152,156,173,177,205

File.Exists(String) Method 152,205

FileAccess 126,205

FileAccess.Read 128,205

FileAccess.Write 125,205

FileMode 205

FileMode.Open 128,205

Flowchart 16,17,205

Flush() Method 71,119,136,177,205

Font.Color Property 153,206

Font.Size property (Word) 153,206

For Each Loop 57,65,84,183,184,206

For Each...Next 206

For Loop 57,62,63,64,65,84,88,202,206

For...Next 206

Form 10,161-169,173,178,183,206

Format() Method 153,177,206

Format.SpaceAfter property (Word) 153,
    206

Forms Applications 161,162,164,206,208

Function Statement 206

G

GetInstalledVoices (SpeechSynthesizer)

183,207

H

Handles Clause 177,185,207
High-level programming language 207

I

IDE 6,18,160,207,208,210
Identifiers 101,207,211
If 53,54,65,99,129,136,150,152,182-186,207
If...Then...Else 54,207
Imports 71,118,124,170,182,207
Information 7,29,38,127,151,152,207
Information hiding 5,204,207
Inheritance 31,207,210
Instance 6,31,35-38,43,44,72,107,118,120,
          124,125,126,137,139,151,200,202,
          203,207,210
Instantiate 38,42,107,137,182,183,202,208
Integer 19,23,25,34,56,73,76,88,114,150,
          185,208
Integrated Development Environment 6,
                    208,210
Internal Memory 22,208
Interpreter 12,13,139,208
IsNot 74,76,183,184,208
Items.Add Method 177,184,208
Iteration Iteration 49,57,208

L

Label Control 162,208
LinkLabel Control 162,208
List() 107,184,208
ListBox Control 162,179,209
ListBox.Items Property 209
ListView Control 163,209
Logical Operators 75,209
Long 19,209
Loop Statement 57,203,209

M

Machine code 13,209,209

MaskedTextBox Control 163,209

Me 35,209

MessageBox Class 183,209

MessageBox.Show Method 183,209

Method 5,35,36,37,39,43,46,101,108,112, 185,210

Microsoft Visual Studio 6,13,210

Module 43,106,107,108,210

Module Statement 210

Monospaced font 174,210

MonthCalendar Control 163,210

MouseButtons.Right 185,210

MouseDown 185,210

MouseEventArgs 185,210

MsgBox function 186,210

MsgBoxResult.Yes 186,210

MyBase 210

MyBase.Load 210

N

Name property 35,153,166,169,211

Namespace 30,31,43,71,118,161,211

New 34,35,38,42,72,102,120,125,211

Next 62,64,206,211

Non-primitive data types 19,20,211

Nothing 53,61,139,141,183,184,211

NotifyIcon Component 163,211

Numeric variables 25,211

NumericUpDown Control 163,211

O

Object 5,6,19,28,31,35-38,42,71,74,88,107, 118,137,142,185,197-199,202,203, 207,208, 211

Object oriented language 5,212

Of Clause 212

OpenTextFileReader 71,119,212

OpenTextFileWriter 71,212

Operating System 22,212

Operator 77,147,148,212
Operator Precedence 76,212

P

Paragraphs.Add method (Word) 152,212
Parameters 6,24,34,35,37-39,41,88,98,108,
        114,139,185,212
Pascal Casing 101,212
Path.Combine 151,213
Pause Method (SpeechSynthesizer) 179,
        183,184,213
PictureBox Control 163,213
Polymorphism 31,213
Presentations.Open(PowerPoint) 156,213
Preserve 95,213
Primitive data types 19,213
Private 34,213
Procedure 5,6,38,39,41-43,206,212,213
Programming language 5,9,12,38,49,212,
        213,216
ProgressBar Control 163,213
Project 30,165,171,195,213
Properties 31,35-37,73,129,166,168,169,
        177,185,207,214
Public 39,41,42,124,214

R

RadioButton Control 163,214
Range.Font property (Word) 153,214
Range.Font.Bold Property (Word) 153,
        214
Range.InsertParagraphAfter method
        (Word) 153,214
Range.Text property (Word) 152,214
Readkey().KeyChar 94,136,150,214
ReadToEnd() 71,72,119,120,214
Real Numbers 25,214
Record 67,68,128,136,205,214,216
ReDim 95,213,214

Return Statement 38,39,48,95,111,114,
115,150,215
Return values 215
RichTextBox Control 163,182,185,215
Run Command (for WshShell) 137,139,
215

S

Scope 106,107,215
Scripting language 215,221
Select Case Statement 148,149,215
Selection 49,52,54,148,149,215
SelectVoice 182,215
Semantics 15,215
Sender parameter 215
Sentinel value 94,215
Sequence 49,50,215
Sequential file 121,124,166,216
SetSelected Method 184,216
Shared Statement 46,47,84,87,88,95,111,
114,115,216
SlideMaster.CustomLayouts 156,216
Slides.AddSlide 157,216
Slides.Count 157,216
Solution 105,216
Solution Explorer 169,216
SpeakAsync 182,216
Speaking (SpeechSynthesizer) 183,216
SpeechSynthesizer Class 216
Split Method (String) 129,216
State Property (SpeechSynthesizer) 183,
184,217
Step 62,64,65,217
StreamReader 71,72,119,127,129,217
StreamWriter 71,72,118,119,120,126,135,
136,217
String 19,24,34,35,38,41,42,46,56,60,84,87,
88,94,95,115,128,129,151,183,217
Structure Statement 19,29,30,217
Structures 29,217

Sub Statement 41,42,84,217
Sub procedure 211,217
Subscript 88,99,198,217
Syntax 9,15,53,128,149,217
System.IO 71,118,120,218

T

Text property 166,168,182,187,218
Text To Speech 178,179,182,218
TextBox Control 163,218
Then 53,54,65,99,150,207,218
To 62,64,65,115
ToDouble Method 218
ToInt16 56,114,218
ToInt32 126,218
ToolTip Component 163,218
ToString() 129,130,136,177,218
TreeView Control 164,218

U

Ubound Function 88,94,98,218
Unicode 13,139,199,219
Until Statement 57,60,61,99,219
Using 72,120,125,128,195,219

V

Val Method 150,219

Variables 22-30,35,37,41,46,47,48,56,62,
        73,197,211,219
Variable-width font 174,219
Variant Data type 139,141,151,155,219
vbAbort 186,219
vbBack 115,219
vbCancel 186,219
vbCr 115,219
vbCrLf 60,71,115,219
vbFormFeed 115,219
vbIgnore 186,219
vbLf 114,115,219
vbNewLine 115,220

vbNo 187,220
vbNullChar 115,220
vbNullString 220
vbObjectError 115,220
vbOK 187,220
vbRetry 187,220
VBScript 137,202,220
vbTab 115,220
vbVerticalTab 115,220
vbYes 187,210,220
Visible property (Word) 153,155,220
Visual Basic .NET 1,220

W

WebBrowser Control 164,220
While Statement 160,220
Windows Shell 131,135,137,139,141,202,
                221
Workbooks.Add(Object) Method 155,221
Worksheet object (Excel) 155,197,221
WriteLine() 119,221
WshShell 215,221